MW01169275

LEADING WITH CULTURE

BUILDING PEOPLE-CENTRIC HIGH-PERFORMING ORGANIZATIONS

TIMOTHY TIRYAKI, PH.D.

Tellwell Talent
www.tellwell.ca

ISBN
978-1-77962-534-2 (Hardback)
978-1-77962-518-2 (Paperback)
978-1-77962-519-9 (eBook)

TABLE OF CONTENTS

Reviews

"Leading With Culture is full of great ways to help leaders transcend and realize the collective potential of those they serve."

- Scott Barry Kaufman, Ph.D.,
Author of Transcend.

"Grounded in Maslow's hierarchy of needs, Tiryaki offers a deeply human-centered and incredibly practical approach to leading, managing, and changing organizations through culture. Timely and highly relevant for organizations across the globe."

- Jeroen Kraaijenbrink, Ph.D.,
Author of The One-Hour Strategy &
The Strategy Handbook

"Leading With Culture presents a compelling case for culture as a top leadership priority, putting employee needs front and center. It equips leaders with practical strategies to build resilient, high-performing organizations where people thrive."

- Olesya Govorun, Ph.D.,
Organizational Development and
Culture Lead at Pfizer

"More and more organizations are appreciating the importance of culture as a means of creating cohesion, improving collaboration and inspiring high-performance. The question then becomes, 'What can we do to consciously co-create the culture we want for our organization?' Leading with Culture provides great insights into what can be done to influence organizational culture and through practical case studies and challenging suggestions, translates the theory into practical actions accessible to all organizations committed to becoming their best."

- Gord Aker, P.Eng., MCC

"For years, I struggled with the flawed methods of measuring culture in the large organizations I worked for, often feeling frustrated by the imprecise and irrelevant insights that followed. 'Leading with Culture' is an invaluable resource for any leader looking to cultivate teams and organizations that are primed to succeed in the 21st century."

- Didier Périlleux, M.Sc.,
PCC, Vice-President, Pfizer Inc.

"Leading with Culture is a revolutionary text that examines workplace culture in a post COVID-19 context. Through transforming Maslow's Hierarchy of Needs into a system of Hierarchy of Needs at Work, practitioners have an accessible guidebook for improving workplace culture and creating high-performing teams."

- Emma Devonish, JD, Ph.D.,
Executive Coach and Consultant
CCEP, SHRM-CP, and Principal of Creative
Compliance Communication Services, LLC.

ACKNOWLEDGEMENTS

It truly takes a village to bring a book to life, and my village has been nothing short of extraordinary.

At the very heart of this journey is Chloe Tiryaki, my life partner. Chloe, your unmeasurable support, and unwavering belief in me have been the bedrock of not just this book, but my entire journey.

To the incredible team at Maslow, especially Vanessa Raber and Sarah Holman, your detailed reviews and thoughtful suggestions have been invaluable.

To my editors, Michael B. Kinley & Alana Uberig, your keen eyes, and insightful feedback have greatly enriched this work.

My gratitude extends to Mitacs for their generous support through a research grant. This book wouldn't be the same without the crucial data and insights that this grant facilitated.

I am deeply thankful to Diana Serban from St. Mary University's Organizational Psychology Department. Diana, under the expert supervision of Dr. Kevin Galloway, your dedication and expertise in conducting this research have been instrumental in shaping the contents of this book.

Lastly, I owe a world of gratitude to Dr. Heesoon Bai and Dr. Avraham Cohen. As my Ph.D. supervisor and mentor, Dr. Bai, your wisdom, and guidance have been a constant source of inspiration. Dr. Cohen, your encouragement to explore the realms of humanizing leadership and organizations has opened new horizons for me. Your teachings have not only influenced this book but have also profoundly impacted my personal and professional growth.

To each and every one of you, thank you from the bottom of my heart. This book is not just a reflection of my work, but a testament to your support, guidance, and faith in me.

CHAPTER 1

We Need a Way of Looking at Workplace Culture

Introduction: From Change to Transformation

Change is a constant. Yet, there are moments in time where the pace of change accelerates. These significant moments open new chapters in our history. The 21st century workplace was already in flux, trying to adapt to this VUCA environment (volatile, uncertain, complex, and ambiguous). Since the Covid-19 pandemic, there has been a significant transformation in the meaning of work. This is where transformation management comes in.

If change management is managing the continuous, incremental change, transformation management is a strategic intervention of catching up with the accelerated change. Change is evolution; transformation is a revolution.

As much as the Covid-19 pandemic is over, it has accelerated the 21st century's (r)evolution and created a global shift in the meaning making on what work stands for. This book intends to help those interested to understand the culture transformation that organizations and leaders are going through, bringing research-driven findings on how to navigate this next chapter. If your organization is not discussing transformation management and especially the cultural aspects of transformation, I would be seriously concerned.

The employees who left their offices at the start of the pandemic are not the same ones that returned. From the ashes of Covid-19 rose a new social contract of work. What employees need and expect from work is now different; perhaps the needs were always the same, but now people are taking action if their needs are not met at work. They rebel by quitting or by refusing to meet corporate demands that employees feel ignore their concerns and their wishes.

The World Economic Forum (2021) popularized the term the Great Resignation, first proposed by Prof. Klotz from Texas A&M University; other terms defining this social phenomenon are the Great Reshuffle, the Great Attrition, or the Great Quit, which all describe the masses of employees from around the world who have been leaving their jobs, by choice, to find more humane organizations and leaders to work for.

Research from Gallup (Harter, 2023) and McKinsey (De Smet, A., et al., 2023) consistently show that most of the workforce is disengaged from their jobs. Meanwhile, leaders are trying to build organizations and teams that deliver results. Leaders are going through a long overdue wake-up call as employees—more accurately, as human beings—are questioning their priorities in life: what they are willing to give to work and most importantly, what they don't want to sacrifice in order to work.

Microsoft's understanding of these trends is summarized in their research "Making Hybrids Work," which defines a new "worth-it equation" that people have formed in their minds (Microsoft, 2022). Rather than a search engine equation, this concept is similar to an algorithm, which calculates whether it's worth staying at a workplace.

In Microsoft's research, there were five things that people were looking for in new jobs, and they were: a positive culture, mental health and wellbeing benefits, a meaningful purpose, flexible work hours, and more than the standard two weeks of vacation per year.

This aligns with the research we conducted at Maslow Research Center to understand the changing hierarchy of needs at work, where our list further specifies the basic needs, the psychological needs and the leadership needs at work. I will explain that new hierarchy as we go and show how we might change it.

The role and responsibilities of the organization and its leaders are shifting and reflect an expectation to take better care of their people. I have had conversations with several leaders who felt like they were expected to parent their employees or be more involved in their personal lives. As difficult as this sounds, this reflects the truth about the expanding scope of leadership. Employees expect the employers to help them with financial decisions, educational decisions, and family decisions. As a result, leaders need to develop their coaching and mentoring skills and learn how to address wellbeing and the whole person at work. Many leaders are not equipped to deal with this side of people management.

This also aligns with the rise in the wellbeing movement, where organizations develop programs and policies to help employees improve their wellbeing. Gallup's Wellbeing at Work (2021) model brings attention to the five pillars of wellbeing: career wellbeing, which is about how satisfied we are with the job we are doing; social wellbeing, which is about the health of our connections with friends and family; physical wellbeing, and how the body's physical health is affected by sleep, nutrition, and physical activity; financial wellbeing, which covers our relationship with money, prosperity, spending, and saving habits; and finally community wellbeing, which is about our connections to a community in which we feel like we belong and to which we contribute.

Leaders are struggling to manage the "people side" of their roles. Many leaders whom I have coached in the last two years confidentially admitted they feel unprepared to handle the influx of people initiatives emerging in their workplaces.

The tension between getting results that satisfy the bottom line and building relationships and trust with their employees is an increasing challenge for leaders. I call this the performance versus people challenge. In the typical dualistic thinking that most of us fall into, many leaders think you can either be results and performance focused or relationship and people focused, but not both at the same time. This is where my work comes in. I work with these leaders to build both people-focused and high-performing organizations. This is the essence of teaching leaders how to lead with culture.

I found that leaders who see people and culture as separate initiatives tend to face exhaustion and frustration. Meanwhile, I found that leaders who build a cohesive understanding on how the operational and people initiatives interconnect and support each other, find greater meaning and experience less burnout.

The leaders who can integrate the meaning of evolving leadership in this new era are the ones driving progress. Yet, leaders and managers have not been properly educated and trained on how to lead with culture or how to coach and mentor employees.

Whether we like it or not, this is happening. Change is inevitable; growth is optional. I wrote this book to help leaders and managers at all levels better understand what is happening, build common language to identify these challenges, and also provide solutions to bridge the gap with the Leading with Culture philosophy and approach.

Culture Eats Strategy for Breakfast. But How?

Many leaders prioritize strategic management and operations management with the main attention on products and services, but the pandemic changed the game. I like reminding leaders that people, culture, and technology are the key competitive advantages of the 21st century. This doesn't take away the product and service focus; rather, bringing the right people together, building a strong culture, and enabling them with the appropriate technology are the foundations of sustainable products, service development and delivery.

The elements of people and culture are two very important parts of leadership which organizations are slowly realizing are critical for their success. The leader has a vital role in building culture in their workplace, and they also have an important role of acting as a mentor and coach for their teams. During Covid-19, I conducted a year-long research study on understanding the changing employee needs in the remote work environment. In the focus groups that we conducted, many leaders were familiar with the famous quote, "culture eats strategy for breakfast" (frequently attributed to Peter Drucker yet the literature lacks an exact citation of this). Almost everyone acknowledged the importance of culture, but a more balanced view might be that strategy and culture are interrelated and interdependent. Culture can become a hindering or a supporting force for realizing the strategy, depending on how it is cultivated and led by leaders.

When I probed further into how leaders led with and managed culture, many leaders looked for their HR leaders' cues. We have lots of work to do on building literacy and language to equip leaders with a holistic understanding of culture, their toolkits, and how to be a role model of culture. Most leaders refer to the corporate North Star as culture, which is a great starting point. However, we need to help them understand that culture is more than just the values on the wall. Educating leaders on how to lead with culture is the missing link in building the culture they want to see in their organizations.

Culture is not something that only HR is responsible for; the leader has an immense responsibility to build culture in the workplace. The problem is that they don't have the training on this immensely complex topic. They couldn't answer how culture eats strategy for breakfast, because they simply didn't know enough about culture's appetite. And, truly, how can we expect them to know if we are not helping them understand what it means to lead with culture?

Culture needs to be acknowledged as part of the strategic plan; the two are interrelated and work together. Leaders at all levels need to have culture on their agenda, and they are responsible for role modeling it. Culture needs to be measured and integrated into the leaders' actions plans. Leaders need to create space for their teams to have rituals and develop collaboration and cooperation techniques. All these things contribute to their workplace culture. It's the leaders' responsibility to build team culture, and that happens from understanding needs.

In summary, leading with culture means:

- Culture is part of the strategic plan: there is a specific item on people and culture or employee experience in the core strategy, hence culture is not just left to HR.
- Culture is measured and managed with KPIs (key performance indicators): instead of lagging measures of retention or turnover, leaders use leading measures such as the Culture-Actualization Index© presented in this book,

and there are goals for these proactive, leading measures.

- Culture is part of the leaders' agendas (in their action plans): leaders personally role model culture, lead, and sponsor culture initiatives. All people managers at all levels have people and culture initiatives on their agenda.

- Leaders/managers are educated on how to lead with culture: training focuses on building common language, helping leaders understand what is within their control and describes levers that leaders can work on to build a great workplace culture.

- Leaders/managers are supported with coaching to role model culture: leaders are educated on coaching but also receive a specific type of coaching. This new field of coaching, called Organizational Culture Coaching©, will be defined later in this book

A New Definition of Workplace Culture

Culture is a complex topic that comes from anthropology and can be described as values and behaviors that contribute to unique social and psychological environments. It's based on shared attitudes, beliefs, customs, language, symbols, and written or unwritten rules that have been developed over time.

For organizations, in simple terms, workplace organizational culture is about how we collaborate and cooperate as human beings. It's our shared way of being and doing, a constellation of behaviors rooted in mindsets and habits.

In terms of culture management, organizations mostly focus on the company's values and the behaviors that demonstrate them. Ideally these are integrated into performance management, learning and development, and career planning. However, in many cases there are significant gaps and disconnects.

At Maslow Research Center, we are redefining the way workplace culture is understood. There are three facets of culture that leaders need to understand:

- **Culture as a North Star – Inspirational/ Aspirational Culture:** The organization's framework of purpose, vision, mission, values, goals, and ambitions. The North Star ideally also includes an employee value proposition, which also clarifies the culture strategy.
- **Culture as an Operational Fabric – Operational Culture:** Operational culture pertains to shared ways of working, strategy execution, meeting protocols, and day-to-day practices. It's the culture in the operations, how systems are used, and how policies and procedures are executed. In simple terms, it's how the phones are answered, and the boxes are moved.
- **Culture as Employee Experience – Lived/ Experienced Culture:** This facet delves into the firsthand experiences of employees: the reality of culture on the ground. While companies may develop policies, procedures, and processes

aligned with their values, the actual employee experience often reveals gaps.

The Leading With Culture© Approach

Many leaders perceive culture as a North Star, whereas an employee's perception is culture as lived experience. In my opinion, this gap is one of the main reasons for the Great Resignation and quiet quitting; leaders don't understand the employee's perspective. As much as we teach leaders about emotional intelligence and empathy, it's clear that this approach doesn't suffice. We must educate them on employee experience from a needs perspective.

This is the heart of empathy: understanding the employee experience through the lens of their needs. As we continue to research this area and develop the most comprehensive approach to workplace culture management, this book shares research findings on culture as employee experience, which takes a Maslowian, employee needs-based perspective, shaping the Hierarchy of Needs at Work, Maslow 2.0. In this latest addition, it also explores our research findings on operational culture, which focuses on how the systems and structure of an organization shapes its culture.

The Missing Piece: Culture As a North Star

Culture as a North Star is one facet of our holistic approach to measuring culture. It focuses on the organization's purpose, mission, and goals.

My understanding of this aspect of organizational culture started by asking one question: what do Fortune 500 companies value the most?

After reviewing the corporate values of 100 leading organizations, I conducted a cluster analysis to group similar values together. The results highlight the core principles that are driving businesses today. These values serve as the foundation for creating sustainable, people-centered, and high-performing organizations.

Below are the key clusters identified:

Integrity

Integrity remains the cornerstone of corporate ethics. It's more than just doing the right thing—it's about fostering trust internally and externally by maintaining ethical standards across all business dealings.

Customer Focus/Client-Centeredness

Successful companies prioritize their customers by placing their needs and satisfaction at the forefront of decision-making. Whether called customer focus or client-centeredness, this value drives long-term loyalty and brand trust.

Innovation/Future Orientation

Innovation is essential for maintaining competitiveness in today's fast-paced world. Companies with a future-oriented mindset encourage continuous exploration, creativity, and adaptability to ensure sustained growth and industry leadership.

Excellence

Excellence is about striving for the highest standards in all aspects of business. It involves a commitment to quality, performance, and improvement, ensuring that organizations remain leaders in their industries.

Accountability/Ownership

Ownership and accountability define organizations that value responsibility and transparency. These companies empower their teams to take initiative and own the outcomes, leading to a culture of trust and higher performance.

Teamwork/Collaboration

The power of teamwork and collaboration cannot be understated. This value encourages companies to foster environments where individuals work together towards common goals, driving innovation and improving outcomes.

Continuous Improvement

Continuous improvement is critical. Companies embracing this mindset focus on constantly enhancing processes, products, and skills to stay ahead of the curve.

Care/Social Responsibility/Sustainability

Social responsibility, care for others, and sustainability are increasingly important values. These organizations take proactive steps to positively impact society and the environment, ensuring they contribute to a better future for all.

Respect

Respect for individuals—whether employees, customers, or partners—is foundational to maintaining a positive workplace culture. It fosters mutual understanding, open communication, and inclusivity.

Trust

Trust is the glue that holds businesses together. Whether between colleagues, customers, or stakeholders, trust underpins successful collaboration and long-term relationships, creating a resilient and cohesive organization.

These are the most frequently observed values in organizations. Here's the catch: defining and announcing these is one thing, but living up to them is another.

Our research on employee needs revealed that a key expectation employees have is to work for leaders who serve as role models—both in exemplifying organizational values and in their personal lives. This raises the bar for leadership, as leaders must understand how their actions, words, and even inactions shape workplace culture. This is where culture coaching becomes essential. It helps leaders align their behavior with the organization's values, fostering a stronger, more cohesive culture.

While we have researched and created tools for the other two facets, operational culture (the Operational Culture Index©) and employee needs (the Culture-Actualization Index©), culture as North Star is the next element we will continue to explore and further refine.

The North Star framework will delve deeper into the intricate relationship between strategy and culture, specifically examining the alignment (or lack thereof) in key areas such as organizational purpose, vision, and core values. By exploring these dimensions, our research aims to offer a more nuanced understanding of how strategic goals and cultural dynamics influence each other. This initiative will complement the insights from the CAI and OCI, filling gaps in our current models and providing a clearer path to improving overall organizational performance.

As the North Star framework continues to be developed, this book will focus on the current tools we have developed to examine operational culture and employee needs in workplace culture.

The Heart of EQ and Empathy: Human Experience and Needs

In any type of workplace problem, it is impossible to discard the element of human nature. It's our lack of understanding and curiosity about human nature that contributes to so many of the complexities we face, both in the workplace and in the world.

We don't have to be psychologists to understand people. We simply need to be curious, ask, listen, and learn. What I have noticed is that great leaders, salespeople, HR practitioners, doctors, teachers—great people, really—understand human psychology. The importance of understanding the people around you cannot be overstated.

Daniel Goleman's Emotional Intelligence (EQ) framework consists of the intersection of the self and others dimensions, along with the awareness and management dimensions. From these come four quadrants: self-awareness, self-management, social awareness, and relationship management. There have since been several expansions of the EQ model, yet the essence of this framework remains. Being aware of the self and others and understanding how to manage yourself and relationships is a timeless, wise insight.

When compared to Howard Gardner's (1993) multiple intelligences theory, EQ is very similar to intrapersonal intelligence—the ability to understand one's own thoughts, feelings, and emotions (introspection)—and interpersonal intelligence—being able to understand others' perspectives and emotions.

A great leader possesses strong emotional, intrapersonal, and interpersonal intelligence; they enable you to understand and display empathy: our ability to look from other's perspectives. Many leaders can describe what empathy is, but not demonstrate it in action. Knowing the concept of empathy is very different from actively practicing it.

Some leaders think they are showing empathy because they demonstrate the golden rule of ethics: "treat others how you want to be treated." When you start to understand relationality and human needs together, the 21st century shift to the platinum rule "treat others how *they* want to be treated" starts to make a lot more sense.

This simple shift is what describes the changing leadership paradigm—leaders need to understand employee needs to create a shared collective synergy. Demonstrating empathy is not about assuming; rather, it is about asking, listening, hearing, and learning about the person with whom you communicate. If a leader is struggling with practicing empathy, the problem likely lies in the failure to understand the other person's needs. The leader's needs, the other person's needs, and the collective needs are all equally important. Leaders can cultivate emotional intelligence and enhance their capacity for empathy by adopting this needs-based way of thinking.

Redefining Servant Leadership

A senior-level leader in a Fortune 500 company approached me for coaching. She took pride in being a servant leader, striving to work alongside her team and actively participate in the collaboration process. In her mind, she was being selfless. However, she started receiving feedback that she was limiting people's growth, wasn't supportive, and poorly delegated tasks.

During our coaching sessions, this leader expressed frustration at the feedback, as she couldn't pinpoint the reason behind it. But once we began examining the culture and context of her workplace, the cause of the disconnect became clear.

She viewed herself as an equal partner to her team since they were also senior-level, but she was still their boss. She wanted to collaborate and work alongside them, with no intention of misusing her authority—she truly believed her approach was helpful. However, whenever she presented an idea in meetings, her team hesitated to debate, suggest alternatives, or share their experiences because she was their leader. It felt illogical or risky for the team to do anything but agree. Although she saw herself as an equal, her team still saw her as their superior. In this situation, her needs were met, but the collective team's needs were not.

We needed to redefine her concept of servant leadership. This meant prioritizing the team's needs over her own. The best way for her to serve them was to step back from the meetings, set clear boundaries, and trust her team, empowering them in a way that worked for everyone.

Her intentions were good, but her lack of understanding of her team's needs had caused an issue. After several coaching sessions and adopting a different approach to servant leadership, she found herself more aligned with her team. She became their coach and transitioned into a more strategic role. Her adaptability, a needs-based approach, and coaching contributed to the team's ultimate success.

From Measuring Engagement to Measuring Employee Experience

Up until the 1990s, there were measurements on employee satisfaction. Then researchers decided they needed something more reliable and robust, so the focus shifted to employee engagement. The concept of it took a while to stick, but once they learned how to measure it, it was a useful tool in organizations.

Companies with high employee engagement typically have positive outcomes. However, when you look at the employee engagement trends in the last twenty years, the percentage of engaged and disengaged employees has remained relatively stagnant. As of 2023, the percentage of engaged employees at work varies between 20%-40% based on different studies. Clearly, disengagement is the dominant paradigm in today's workforce. I have also seen leaders who quickly label employees as disengaged but fail to do the work to understand why they are disengaged.

When an employee has prolonged unmet needs, they naturally become disengaged. For example, when employers fail to involve an employee consistently throughout their career or neglect their development, leaders cannot expect that an employee will be engaged or satisfied in their role; in this instance, disengagement is the inevitable result. We need to shift our focus to understanding and measuring the root causes of engagement. It centers around the employee experience and how the employers meet—or don't meet—their employees' needs.

Gallup defines employee engagement as the involvement and enthusiasm of employees in their work and workplace (2023). I interpret and rephrase this definition as the employees' commitment to their work. Yet an organization might have committed employees who are not flourishing or actualizing.

Bringing the language of needs and actualization to the forefront allows for a much more comprehensive way of measuring and making employee experience the new evaluation measure. Many leaders still see experience as subjective and wonder how we could effectively measure it, yet the same could have been said about satisfaction and engagement. We need a new way of measuring culture, managing culture, and helping leaders build a common language of culture. That is why I developed the Leading with Culture© approach, which brings together culture assessment, action planning and coaching as complimentary pieces supporting culture transformation.

To understand employee experience as human needs, we need to go back to one of the thought leaders of humanistic psychology, Abraham Maslow, and his theory of motivation. As I briefly review Abraham Maslow's work on motivation and needs, I will move into how I reconceptualized Maslow's Hierarchy of Needs for the 21st century, post-Covid-19 workplace, creating the new hierarchy of employee experience at work.

CHAPTER 2

Employee Experience from a Maslowian Perspective

Maslow's Hierarchy of Needs: An Overview

Abraham Maslow was one of the most cited psychologists of the 20th century and one of the founding fathers of humanistic psychology. He introduced a theory in the mid-20th century that sought to explain human motivation through a hierarchy of needs. The theory, popularly known as Maslow's Hierarchy of Needs, posits that human beings have a series of innate needs that they strive to satisfy in a specific order. The hierarchy is typically represented as a pyramid, with basic needs at the bottom and higher-level needs at the top.

1. Physiological Needs

These are the basic biological necessities for human survival. Without these, the human body cannot function optimally. Physiological needs include air, food, drink, shelter, clothing, warmth, and sleep.

2. Safety Needs

This level encompasses both physical safety and emotional security and includes concepts such as protection, security, order, law, stability, and freedom from fear.

3. Social Needs (Love and Belonging)

Humans are inherently social creatures, and we have a need of belonging and feeling love. This sense of belonging to a family or community brings both safety and also a sense of identity. Social needs can be met through relationships with others in which we receive trust, acceptance, affection, and love.

4. Esteem Needs

Esteem needs revolve around gaining recognition, status, importance, and respect from others. There are two types of esteem needs: esteem for oneself (dignity, achievement, mastery, independence) and the desire for reputation or respect from others (status, prestige). The evolution of this need is from outside-in, external esteem towards feeling esteem internally, without external validation. Some examples are a sense of achievement, mastery, independence, status, dominance, prestige, self-respect, and respect from others.

5. Self-Actualization Needs

This is the pinnacle of Maslow's hierarchy. At this level, individuals are focused on personal growth, self-fulfillment, and reaching their potential. They seek to realize their own abilities and strive to become the best version of themselves. Understanding one's North Star; seeking purpose; and pursuing inner talent, creativity, fulfillment, and personal growth are examples of how a person might attempt to satisfy this type of need.

It's worth noting that Maslow later added a sixth level above self-actualization, termed "self-transcendence." This involves connecting to a higher purpose or cause beyond oneself, which could include spiritual or altruistic pursuits. As my focus in this book and my work is primarily the workplace, I will leave this topic for another book.

Since its introduction, Maslow's hierarchy has been applied in a variety of fields, including business, education, and healthcare, as a framework for understanding motivation and personal development. However, the model has not been without criticism. Some argue that the hierarchy is too simplistic and does not take into account cultural differences. For instance, in some societies, communal or societal needs might take precedence over individual needs. Additionally, the strict progression through the hierarchy has been questioned, with some suggesting that individuals might not strictly follow the sequence or that needs from different levels can be pursued simultaneously.

Although common language on the Hierarchy of Needs share that each level of the pyramid must be satisfied before an individual can move on to the next level, Maslow in his later work acknowledges how the needs are dynamic and sometimes interrelated, but continuously ebb and flow.

Regardless of its criticisms, Maslow's Hierarchy of Needs has left a lasting mark on the field of psychology and beyond. It provides a structured lens through which we can understand human motivation and the factors that drive our actions. Whether you see it as a strict progression or a flexible framework, the hierarchy sheds light on the multifaceted nature of human needs and aspirations.

As I took a deeper dive into Abraham Maslow's personal journals and unpublished manuscripts, I discovered a visionary who wanted to help all humanity towards realizing our collective potential. His efforts to define characteristics of self-actualization are as valuable as his work on the Hierarchy of Needs. In addition, his definitions of Deficiency Needs (D-Needs) and Being Needs (B-Needs) clearly illustrate the existential tension we all experience between life's dilemmas. On one side we feel pulled towards an inner calling of who we are or who we can be (B-Needs). On the other, there are needs that tend to hold us back with an unending cycle of craving or attachment to safety, security, and societal expectations (D-Needs).

I take pride in being inspired by Maslow and continuing his work on building self-actualizing individuals, teams, and organizations, as I have proposed a new term in the literature: culture-actualization.

The Self-Actualization and Culture-Actualization Loop

If self-actualization is the realization of an individual's potential or talent, then culture-actualization is the realization of a workplace's potential through their employees. Culture-actualization means helping individuals and teams meet their basic, psychological, and leadership needs, moving towards self-actualization collectively.

These two concepts—self-actualization and culture-actualization—are highly intertwined. Everyone is part of a community (unless you are choosing to live a secluded life on your own, disconnected from society). Even monks, meditating on rural mountains, are part of a community of monks and their cultural tradition. If we want to reach our self-actualization while being part of an organization and a community, we need to understand that the organization's actualization and our own are intertwined.

Many leaders see organizations as machines. "An organization should be a well-oiled machine," is still the dominant paradigm, where people are expenses, but machines and equipment are assets. The truth is an organization is a living organism. We are like the cells of a tissue or organ in a body.

You can't achieve culture-actualization without incorporating self-actualization, since a culture is made of individuals; you cannot thrive as a group if everyone is not also thriving as an individual. This is a key finding of our research, and we model culture and self-actualization as an interdependent continuum. This is one of the biggest perspective changes that I am helping leaders to truly internalize.

This is also a mindset training program. Many leaders know about systems thinking, yet when they need to show the ability to move between the levels of the system (the whole organization, the business unit, the teams, and the individuals), most fail to empathize. As leaders build their knowledge on human needs in the workplace, they will understand employee experience and will be able to empathize, coach, mentor, and lead the system better.

The lack of understanding of human nature and the inability to meet employees' needs is at the core of many workplace problems. Organizations must shift their focus to meeting human needs to create people-centered, high-performing workplace cultures. Emotional intelligence, the employee-client experience continuum, coaching and mentorship practices, and the evolution of performance evaluation practices (among many other factors) all play a part in a company's success in creating a thriving culture. It's also important to consider these topics from multicultural and DEI perspectives, as needs and safety look different depending on the context and audience.

To truly understand employee experience, it's essential to recognize the value of various segments within the organization—not only as business units, but also as diverse demographics. This includes not just age and gender, but also cognitive and behavioral differences. Identifying toxic leaders and teammates, which we call hotspots, as well as recognizing role model leaders who build great workplace cultures, are both a part of leading with culture.

Some leaders object that "it will never be possible to get 100% on all dimensions, all topics, all demographics of the survey, all the time." This is correct. However, that's not the goal of leading with culture. The goal is to keep culture on the agenda and ensure that, each year, employees are heard and there are genuine, human-centered initiatives that are developed, revised, or updated. It's a continuous improvement cycle of always looking for opportunities to improve by 1%.

The Culture-Actualization Index© Development

It was Abraham Maslow's work on self-actualization and *Eupsychian Management* (later republished as *Maslow on Management*) that inspired me to develop and research the concept of culture-actualization.

I started by asking these questions: What do employees need from their organizations? What motivates them to stay and give their best? This quickly evolved into a direct question: How does Maslow's Hierarchy of Needs (and Alderfer's ERG theory) relate to workplace culture and employee culture?

To develop this new measure of culture as employee experience and to understand the changing employee needs at work, I started by conducting a yearlong qualitative research study through focus groups. This research was conducted under Maslow Research Center and resulted in the Maslow at Work 1.0 framework. Then, we received a research grant and partnered with St. Mary University's Organizational Psychology department for further quantitative research and validation. Those interested in understanding the research process can review the appendix section on the research.

The early findings quickly spread during the end of the pandemic, and since then several large organizations have brought our work into their leadership development programs and culture initiatives. Some have institutionalized the leading with culture philosophy and the Culture-Actualization Index©.

The Culture-Actualization Index© has three areas of measurements derived from our research: basic, psychological, and leadership needs. By the end of this book, you'll understand exactly what culture-actualization is and why using this framework will be the competitive advantage for organizations today.

Maslow's Hierarchy Redesigned

It has been almost 80 years since Maslow established the original theory of motivation, the progression of needs. Very few know that Abraham Maslow never visualized his work as the pyramid. It was Charles McDermid who popularized that design in the 1960s as a tool for consultants. Maslow's work was much more nuanced than the simple triangle that has been illustrated throughout the latter half of the 20th century. This insufficient context has led to vast misinterpretation of his model.

For example, many think the Hierarchy of Needs represents a linear process, like a video game where you unlock the next level as you move forward. Although Maslow's writings in early expressions of his theory imply some linearity, in most of his work he acknowledges the dynamic relationship between needs and how they come from a progression and regression, with simultaneous needs acting together. We cannot assume that completion of one need or level means automatic progression to the next, as this is not the human experience. We often feel multiple needs at once.

Upon considering the way the 21st century has evolved, the Hierarchy of Needs was due for an update, leveraging everything we knew about needs and actualization in 2023. McDermid's pyramid represents 20th century thinking, which is more hierarchical and linear.

I envisioned the hierarchy of needs at work through a model of concentric circles representing circular and holistic thinking, instead of a linear approach. I believe this better represents what Maslow was trying to convey. It also better represents the process of growing as a human being, as it allows for interconnectedness, for stepping out of our comfort zone and for reaching out to the farther limits of our potential.

The visual design, based on the research, acknowledges the complexity of human needs and human nature, understanding that the cycle can weave in and out of the layers depending on personal circumstances. All layers work together, ebb and flow, and are intrinsically connected.

The New Hierarchy of Needs at Work

The results of our analysis allowed us to clearly define the components of a new hierarchy of needs at work, and also brought the opportunity to measure culture as employee experience from a needs perspective. We identified twenty-six needs across three components: basic, psychological, and growth needs.

Basic Needs

The statements in this category are about the employees' needs based on their relationship with the organization. Items include job security, onboarding, tools and technology, compensation and benefits, training, the workplace environment, wellbeing, networking, inclusion, and employee consideration.

Psychological Needs

These statements are about the employees' needs based on their relationship with their colleagues. Items include camaraderie, organizational belonging, and positive interactions.

Growth Needs

These statements are about the employees' needs based on their relationship with their leaders. All items correspond to the leaders' role in the organization and include purpose broadcasting, leadership and values role modeling, clear goal setting, cohesiveness, inclusive decision making, belief in potential, constructive feedback, and their role as a coach and mentor.

We tested a variety of statements for each one of these layers, seeking to understand whether these needs are influenced by the organization, their peers, their immediate supervisor, or something else. The analysis revealed that each one of these layers of needs points to a different relationship. The basic needs are about the employees' relationship to the organization, how the organization meets or does not meet their basic needs; the psychological needs are about the employees' relationship to their peers and the community; and finally, the growth needs are all about the employees' relationship with their direct supervisor.

Maslow's Workforce Hierarchy of Needs©

Growth Needs
Leadership & Values Role Modeling - Clear Goal Setting - Purpose Broadcasting - Constructive Feedback - Inclusive Decision Making - Belief in Potential - Mentoring - Coaching - Cohesiveness

Psychological Needs
Positive Interactions - Belonging - Camaraderie

Basic Needs
Networking - Inclusivity - Creative, Clean, Safe Workspace - Consideration - Wellbeing - Compensation - Benefits - Tools & Technology - Training - Onboarding - Job Security

© Timothy Tiryaki

Based on Leading With Culture (2024)

Most Important Changes on Human Needs at Work

Here are the top findings from our research:

1) The basic needs of employees have increased. Employees have more expectations and higher base expectations from their employers. This might not surprise many employers. We have been able to identify the new list of basic needs at work, which will be discussed in the next chapter.

2) Job security and onboarding are the most basic human needs at work. Employees prioritize organizations that offer job security and a great onboarding process. In my experience, many organizations miss the mark on the onboarding process.

3) Inclusion and wellbeing have evolved from being psychological needs to become basic needs. People want to work for inclusive organizations that care about their wellbeing.

4) Appreciation, recognition, and celebration have shown to not be a significant need in the post-Covid-19 era. This breakthrough finding will challenge many leaders, consultants, and HR practitioners' thinking. Through further focus groups, I found that people value being appreciated and getting a boost of dopamine, but when it's time to decide if this is a significant need, it doesn't affect their decision. Even the customized approaches to show appreciation are

not what count. What matters most is working for great leaders who are great coaches and mentors, who provide constructive feedback, and who believe in the employee's potential.

5) Psychological needs have significantly evolved; they have either become a basic need or have moved up to the growth needs in terms of leadership behaviors.

6) Psychological needs are about belonging, camaraderie, and positive relationships. These are all about relationships with peers. People don't want to work for toxic teams or teams with toxic members, but rather for teams that welcome newcomers and show friendliness and positive communication.

7) Growth needs, which are the highest level of needs for realizing organizational potential, are not about the organization. All the statements that were around the purpose and the mission of the organization dropped off, which means it's no longer the why of the organization that matters. This is one of our most impactful findings: the leader's purpose and their role modeling of the organization's purpose and values are what matter. In simpler terms, people don't want to work for leaders who say one thing and do something else. I captured this one quote from one of the focus groups: "we are sick of working for leaders that don't walk the walk." Leaders are closely evaluated now; employees want to see that leaders know and

live their own North Stars and also, that they role model the organization's North Star.

8) All the growth needs are about one's relationship to their leader. Once more, this is a testimony that leaders make it or break it. The ten statements in our growth index were all about leadership behaviors. In other words, people join organizations but leave managers. These findings are aligned with Gallup's 2019 book It's the Manager, which suggests the best benefits you can offer to your employees are great managers. Employees are looking for wisdom, maturity, and authenticity from their leaders and want to work for leaders who make inclusive decisions. We identified the ten leadership behaviors that drive culture-actualization at work, which will be covered as part of the research findings on the growth needs.

9) Coaching and mentorship are equally important within an organization. Leaders need to learn to develop both coaching skills and mentorship skills, as well as when to use which approach and how to combine these skillsets when necessary. The ability to navigate the coaching and mentorship continuum is going to be one of the critical skillsets.

10) Cohesiveness among leaders was a critical factor. People want to work for organizations where the leaders get along well and work cohesively with each other. Just like kids know when their parents are not getting along, employees can sense when the leaders are pretending to get along and there is a lack of genuine cohesiveness.

We continue to capture new insights as we keep running the Culture-Actualization Index© across different industries and organizations, and we will continue to keep sharing any updated results.

In the updated hierarchy of needs at work, the basic needs create the foundation which an organization builds a great employee experience on. My usage of basic needs brings together Abraham Maslow's first two levels of needs: the physical needs and the security needs. Let's explore how the basic needs have evolved in the 21st century, post-Covid-19 work era. In the next chapters, we will take a deeper dive into the research findings, one finding at a time.

CHAPTER 3

Decoding the Hierarchy of Needs at Work: Basic Needs

In this section of the book, I will further discuss each need we identified and provide example case studies that demonstrate the impact of met and unmet needs. These examples were chosen because they are grounded in real-life situations, but all are fictitious unless otherwise stated. To clarify, I sometimes refer to the research finding as an identified employee need, sometimes as a statement. Both are equivalent, because we have identified twenty-six statistically significant statements that represent an employee need.

The first level, basic needs, are about the employees' relationship to the organization. Our most recent research revealed that employees have higher expectations for their basic needs than previously anticipated. I covered these needs in detail so they can inform both policy makers and also leaders for better relating to employees.

Thirteen statements are considered basic needs, with the two most fundamental needs being onboarding and job security. I encourage organizations taking the survey to also share this book with their managers so they will be able to understand the data better and build culture action plans accordingly.

Basic Need: Onboarding

Statement: My organization has a strong onboarding process.

This need refers to the effectiveness of the onboarding process for new employees or any veteran employees new to their role. It may include clarity of expectations, the support provided during the initial transition period and the integration of new employees into the team or company overall.

Onboarding is a vital cultural practice for any organization. In Microsoft's Work Trend Index 2021, employees with less than a year of experience had some of the lowest scores when it came to wellbeing, and the highest scores indicating their workplace struggles.

These results were largely due to the difficulty organizations encounter in effectively onboarding remote employees. When employees miss out on water cooler opportunities to connect with and learn from their colleagues, it becomes challenging to develop a sense of belonging in the workplace culture.

Having a comprehensive onboarding process is critical. Onboarding can be a rich experience where employees become properly equipped to do their jobs. When done correctly, employees will have access to the necessary equipment and resources, begin building relationships with their colleagues and leaders, have expectations clarified and have their needs met as a result. In contrast, the outdated "sink or swim" approach where new hires are expected to learn by observing the practices of their veteran colleagues, is not effective and is, in fact, an extremely poor onboarding practice.

In my previous experience as an organizational culture consultant, the data analysis of multiple client surveys revealed that a poorly onboarded cohort of employees carried over low levels of trust for two to five years. Employees may not leave the organization during that time, but their work quality and overall wellbeing can suffer. How new hires feel during their onboarding process is essential. If they feel undervalued, stressed, and as if no one cares about them in their new workplace, it can be detrimental to their overall employee experience and so, too, to the organization.

Leaders often overlook the importance of onboarding because they are so busy. However, a poor onboarding experience can have long-lasting negative impacts on the employee and the organization. It is essential to have a well-defined onboarding process that considers the unique challenges faced by remote employees, especially in the post-Covid-19 era. By prioritizing onboarding, organizations can set their employees up for success and ensure their long-term engagement and wellbeing, which is beneficial for everyone.

Case Study

Eliza has just landed her dream job at a large tech company. She is excited to start her new role and contribute her expertise to the company's goals. The position is fully remote and, at first, Eliza likes the idea of remote work because it provides flexibility and allows her to work in her own space. However, her onboarding process quickly lets her down.

On her first day, Eliza logs onto her computer, eager to start. Unfortunately, her supervisor is nowhere to be found. After waiting for an hour and many failed attempts to contact them, Eliza finally receives an email with a generic welcome message and a long list of tasks to complete.

She has been given no access to company tools, no clear expectations, and wasn't even a part of a welcome conversation. She feels confused and overwhelmed, with no clear direction on what to do or who to reach out to for help.

Over the next few weeks, Eliza struggles to connect with her colleagues and understand the company culture. She attends virtual meetings and is introduced to many people, but never given an opportunity to genuinely connect with them.

She can't remember anyone's names, and she doesn't contribute to meetings because she feels like it will disrupt the conversation. When she does reach out to connect with colleagues or for help, her messages often go unanswered. She feels like she is bothering them. As more time passes, Eliza questions whether she is the right fit for the company. At times, the expectations for her role are still unclear and she has questions that, despite her efforts, remain unanswered. She wonders if her colleagues and supervisor even care about her success. She feels stressed, anxious, and alone.

Eliza doesn't want to leave the company; this is her dream job! She knows it is a great opportunity and doesn't want to give up. However, her productivity begins to suffer, and she finds it hard to focus on her work. Her inner conversation is full of self-doubt and frustration.

She feels like just a number in a sea of employees. She wishes that the organization had a clear onboarding process that made new employees, like her, feel welcome and excited to contribute. Instead, she feels invisible.

What You Can Do

- Develop a comprehensive onboarding plan: This plan should include everything from introductions to colleagues, to training on the company's processes and tools. Having a well-structured onboarding plan will ensure that your new remote employee feels welcomed and fully integrated into the team.
- Use video conferencing for virtual introductions: Schedule virtual introductions with the team and other colleagues. Video conferencing platforms such as Zoom or Google Meet can be used for this purpose.
- Provide access to company resources: Provide your new remote employee with access to all necessary company resources such as email, document sharing, project management tools, etc. Ensure that they have all the necessary information to perform their job effectively.

- Assign a mentor or buddy: Assign a mentor or buddy to your new remote employee. This person can be responsible for answering any questions they may have, providing guidance and helping them navigate the company culture.
- Create a virtual company tour (if not entirely remote): Create a virtual tour of the company's office and introduce the remote employee to the different departments and teams. This will give them a sense of the company's culture and environment.
- Schedule regular check-ins: Schedule regular check-ins with your remote employee to monitor their progress and provide feedback. This will help ensure that they are adjusting well and getting the support they need.
- Find ways to add personal touches to a remote world: Sending swag bags, getting lunch delivered to your new hire's home, etc., can be meaningful ways to make them feel welcome.

Basic Need: Job Security

Statement: My job is secure at my organization.

This need/statement assesses whether employees feel confident in their job stability and employment status within the organization. It may include factors such as job performance, the overall financial health of the company and the likelihood of layoffs or restructuring.

Job security is a fundamental need for employees, as it provides them with a sense of stability and predictability. Organizations can meet this need by providing clear communication and transparency about an employee's position in the company, especially during times of change or uncertainty.

This includes providing employees with information about company performance, plans for the future, and any potential impacts on their jobs. Leaders can also support their employees by offering opportunities for upskilling and reskilling, which can increase job security by enhancing employees' skill sets and making them more valuable to the organization.

By prioritizing job security, organizations can create a more stable and positive work environment for their employees, which can lead to higher levels of job satisfaction, engagement, and retention.

Case Study

Andre is a single dad. He supports two young kids who are involved in extracurriculars. He also has a mortgage, pays for afternoon childcare, and puts money away monthly for his children's education.

He works for a distributing company as a warehouse manager, and with his income he can easily support his kids and his own lifestyle. However, Andre recently overheard a conversation some senior level executives were having in the break room on their monthly visit. The interaction sounded tense, and when Andre walked in, they abruptly ended their conversation. The next day, Andre overhears some small talk on the warehouse floor.

"Those executives have been coming by more often," one employee notes.

"I heard they are getting ready to do some layoffs," another commented.

Like his colleagues, Andre has also noticed that the executives have been coming by more often. As warehouse manager, he oversees shipping and receiving and noticed that the price of several goods had gone up, while the quantity of outgoing items had gone down.

He is curious about the financial stability of the company but does not have access to any of that information. The company has never shared their overall performance with the employees, so it feels wrong to ask.

Over the next few weeks, Andre's concern continues to grow. His emails to executives about training and development programs, as well as inquiries about people and culture initiatives within the workplace, go unanswered or pushed off until next year. The company has always been very adamant and progressive about these programs, and their lack of action makes Andre worry.

On their next visit, Andre finally has the courage to ask the executives why they have been coming by more often, and if the organization was struggling financially. They give him a vague, almost scripted answer telling him not to worry. Andre feels worse having asked.

The possibility of him losing his job causes him stress and anxiety, especially when thinking about the wellbeing of his children and their lifestyle. Andre's left wondering if he can rely on his job and his income. Furthermore, when his employees come and ask him about the stability of their jobs, he doesn't have an answer for them. Andre is slowly losing confidence in the company and is disappointed by their lack of communication.

What You Can Do

- Communicate openly and honestly: Employers should be transparent with their employees about the company's plans, goals, and challenges. This can help build trust and foster a sense of community within the organization.
- Provide development opportunities: Employees who receive training or development will feel more secure in their role because the company has invested time and money into them. This will further assure them that they have a place in the company and their jobs are valuable.
- Foster a positive work environment: A supportive and positive work environment can help employees feel comfortable and engaged in their work, which can lead to greater job satisfaction and a sense of security.

Basic Need: Tools and Technology

Statement: My organization provides me with the tools & technology I need to do my job.

This need/statement assesses whether employees feel that they have the necessary resources and equipment to perform their job effectively. It may include items such as computers, software, and other specialized tools, as well as appropriate user training.

Many companies are supporting employees working from home—do they have the right workspace, and are they ergonomically supported? Is their Wi-Fi speed sufficient for their work demands? Who pays for these? The conversation has changed from just having working technology to including remote work and what that means in terms of setup.

In the world we live in, technology is everywhere. It's important that the technology in the workplace supports the work the employees are doing. Out-of-date software, a bad internet connection, faulty hardware, and lack of technical support are among the many difficulties that technology can cause for employees.

When the tools and technology that are meant to facilitate their work actually hinder it, employees are left feeling discouraged and frustrated.

It is also important to provide proper training on tools and technology in the workplace. To assume that employees know how to use all the technology in your workplace can be detrimental to their overall experience and productivity; they may feel underqualified and undervalued. By prioritizing tools and technology in the workplace as well as opportunities for training, employees will be better equipped to do their jobs.

Case Study

Taylor works in a post-secondary institution as an advisor for students. In this role, they act as a resource for students who have questions or need advice.

It's the middle of exam season, and they have been receiving lots of inquiries. Taylor's office upgraded their computer software and migrated to a new email platform. It is one that they have never used before, and the entire interface looks foreign. The first day using the platform, Taylor struggles to find their previous email threads, so they reach out to their colleagues for help.

There was no training on the new system for anyone in the office, so Taylor's request for assistance was unsuccessful. Taylor keeps all the information for upcoming meetings in their emails, and because they can't access the links, they will be late for or even miss their first meeting.

Stressed, they watch YouTube tutorials to try and figure out the problem. Through trial and error, Taylor is able to access their emails and get to their meetings, although much later than scheduled.

The next day, Taylor notices that there aren't any emails in their inbox. This is odd, as typically they will receive dozens of emails overnight from stressed students.

As the day goes by, Taylor's inbox remains empty, which is even more unusual. So, they decide to investigate it. By requesting a colleague to send a test email to their inbox, Taylor discovers that they are not receiving any emails whatsoever.

Stressed and flustered, Taylor begins digging. They find two days' worth of inquiries that have been filtered out due to the new email's security firewall. Taylor is frustrated; if they were properly trained on the new system, they wouldn't be so far behind in their email communication.

Taylor spends the next week trying to catch up on emails, and the workload is overwhelming. They are left wishing that they could still use their previous email platform and disappointed with the company's lack of training.

What You Can Do

- Listen to employees: Ask employees what technology they enjoy using, which ones could use an update and which ones they don't use at all. Conduct focus groups or ethnographic research to understand how employees use (or don't use) technology in their regular workplace settings. Clarity around which tools and technologies are helpful, and taking away excess or bringing in new systems will help boost productivity.
- Develop a clear L&D strategy focusing on upskilling/ reskilling and cross-skilling: Technology training needs to be incorporated in a holistic L&D strategy, built on adult education principles with insights based on company culture. When new technology, tools or online systems are implemented in the workplace, provide training on them. During training, create a safe space and encourage people to ask questions! Many employees will not ask questions about technology features for fear of sounding technologically incompetent, but that's the whole

point of training. If you promote questions, and even create questions that might seem basic, the training environment will be more positive.

- Develop reverse mentoring programs with internal champions: Identify the people who have demonstrated a natural interest and talent in technology who can act as champions and mentors. Be mindful to not just "voluntell" employees and be careful that this doesn't lead to imbalanced workloads. Develop a reverse mentorship program where more comfortable employees can support the ones that need some more guidance. The management and launch of reverse mentorship programs need proper DEI guidance, training, and onboarding.

- Have a space for technology and innovation: Conduct regular team-wide meetings about new tools, trends, and technology that employees have seen in the industry. These conversations can spark new ways of working, encourage the sharing of best practices, and help the team stay up to date with the latest innovations in workplace technology.

Basic Need: Training

Statement: My organization has provided me with the training I need to do my job well.

This need/statement measures whether employees feel they have received the appropriate training and development opportunities to be successful in their role. It may include both initial training when starting a new job, as well as ongoing learning and development opportunities to keep skills up to date.

When we think about training, we mostly think about formal training programs. What we found in our qualitative and quantitative research is that people expect fewer formal in-person and online learning opportunities. Instead, the expectation is to have strong support and training during onboarding and job transition phases, followed by ongoing coaching and mentorship.

While the technology training mentioned in previous needs is also important, the type of training being discussed here centers more around skills and competencies that go beyond tool usage.

Whether an employee is a new hire or has made an internal move in the company, any employee in a new role requires training during their onboarding. Regardless of their previous experience or qualifications, it's unrealistic to assume that they are properly equipped to do their jobs without training. It's also important to upskill and reskill!

As employees continue their career within the company, the workplace, markets, and industries change. Investing in their knowledge and expertise allows employees to broaden their toolkit and improve their understanding of their role.

This often results in a stronger commitment to their quality of work and a better sense of the value they bring to the company. By improving an employee's skills for their long-term career growth, training for career development may encourage them to stay with the company and advance their career within the organization, especially if the training is tailored to their specific goals and aspirations.

Case Study

Mohammed has been working for an insurance company for a few years when he is promoted to team lead. Excited for the opportunity, Mohammed jumps right in. He has had several negative experiences with supervisors in his years at the company, and he is keen to provide his team with great leadership. However, when Mohammed assumes his new role, he isn't given any training.

He thinks it's odd that his new managers don't provide him with training, but he figures it is because they believe in his abilities, so he tries to persevere.

Unfortunately, Mohammed quickly finds himself struggling to manage the team. He doesn't know how to properly delegate tasks or give proper feedback. Despite his attempts, his leadership responsibilities begin to suffer and so does the team's work. Deadlines are missed and emails are left unanswered. Mohammed's team members become frustrated with him.

Eventually, Mohammed's manager realizes that he hasn't provided proper training and support to Mohammed and arranges for him to attend a team management course. Unfortunately, the damage is already done. The team has lost some of its best members, and Mohammed is extremely discouraged. The situation could have been avoided if he had been given proper training and support from the beginning.

Mohammed feels like he doesn't deserve the role. Because of the lack of training, he takes a serious hit to his confidence moving forward.

What You Can Do

- Develop a balanced L&D strategy to support your people and culture goals: Consider any necessary upskilling, reskilling, and cross-skilling for the coming five to ten years and ensure you have the appropriate training plan to support.
- Remember the 70-20-10 rule: We learn 70% through experiences on the job, 20% through social or informal learning (including coaching, mentorship, feedback, and reflective conversations with colleagues and superiors), and only 10% through formal learning.
- Be sure that training programs include onboarding and job transition training plans: For both new hires and internal role changes, having comprehensive training plans is crucial. Organizations should not assume that employees will know how to do their role without any training.
- Have regular check-ins: Evaluate training programs to ensure they are helping employees do their jobs, setting measurable goals, and collecting regular feedback.
- Upskill and reskill: The workforce is continually changing. Organizations need to give employees the opportunity for development and growth to keep up.

Basic Needs: Compensation and Benefits

Statements: I get compensated fairly at work.

I am satisfied with the benefits my organization offers.

These two needs/statements measure whether employees feel they are receiving fair and appropriate compensation for their work, including salary, bonuses, and benefits. It may also include considerations such as the cost of living in the area and how their pay compares to industry standards.

The benefits statement assesses employees' satisfaction with the benefits offered by the organization, such as health insurance, retirement plans, vacation time, and other perks. It may also include consideration of the overall value and competitiveness of the benefits package compared to other companies.

On the benefits side, we are observing important shifts in what employees need. Access to telemedicine and remote doctors is one of the key expectations of employees from their insurance providers. Some employee assistance programs are starting to offer coaching services in addition to counselling services. Keeping the benefits packages updated to the changing needs is an important advantage.

Compensation and benefits are closely related. Employees are not just trading in their time for income; benefits are a significant factor of competitive employment opportunities. In today's job market, a generous benefit package that caters to employee needs can set an organization apart from its competitors. Such benefits may include healthcare coverage, paid time off, employee assistance programs, retirement plans, and other perks.

As pay is becoming more transparent through platforms like Payscale and Glassdoor, and with several US states introducing salary transparency laws, employees expect transparency in pay and a commitment to equity.

With topics like the gender wage gap and racial inequities in income becoming more openly discussed, employees are expecting organizations to take active, intentional steps towards achieving pay equity.

Companies that don't offer fair wages and aren't transparent might find their employees posting their salary information and grievances online. It is a better culture practice to be upfront about pay than forcing your employees to go down unfavorable avenues.

In 2015, the company Salesforce conducted an independent audit to evaluate their pay equity and, much to the CEO's surprise, found a glaring gender gap. Commendably, they spent nearly $9 million to correct this issue and set the stage for other large organizations to move towards a more level playing field.

In this competitive workforce, when employees feel that they are undercompensated, it will likely be reflected in lower productivity as well as higher turnover rates. To attract and retain top talent, organizations need to offer competitive compensation and benefit packages.

Case Study

Aaliyah recently became the Director of People and Culture at her organization, a role she earned through years of hard work and loyalty to the company. However, she feels that her compensation doesn't reflect the value she brings to the company.

With no internal salary or pay scale to reference, Aaliyah researches the market and finds that she is earning significantly less than others in similar roles with comparable skills and experience. Initially, she justifies this by reminding herself of her recent promotion and the enjoyment she gets from her work, assuming that her salary and benefits will eventually increase as she proves herself.

As months go by, Aliyah achieves remarkable results. The people and culture initiatives she leads are thriving, and employee performance is better than ever.

Many employees around her receive salary increases and bonuses, seeing their hard work pay off. Yet, Aaliyah hears nothing about an increase in her pay or benefits package.

When she finally raises the issue with her supervisor, she is told there's no budget for a salary increase in her role. Aaliyah mentions that similar roles in other organizations offer significantly higher pay, and she shares her recent successes demonstrate the value she brings. Her supervisor promises to look into it, but several weeks go by with no update.

Then, Aaliyah learns that another executive in a similar role has received a substantial pay increase, revealing a significant wage gap. She realizes that she is being undervalued.

Over time, Aaliyah's frustration with her compensation begins to affect her work. Her motivation wanes, and the initiatives she leads begin to suffer. Despite her supervisor's feedback and support, the same explanation about the lack of budget is given when she asks again about her compensation and benefits.

Eventually, Aaliyah begins exploring opportunities elsewhere, seeking a role that pays her what she's worth. It doesn't take long before she leaves the company for a position that offers appropriate compensation. The company loses a long-term, loyal employee because they failed to provide competitive pay and benefits.

What You Can Do

- Be transparent: Post your pay bands publicly (or at the very least internally to all employees) so they can see where they fit in the pay scale. This also promotes honesty and prevents uncomfortable workplace whispers about pay.
- Budget for pay equity updates: Dedicate resources and budget to finding and correcting inequities in pay.
- Conduct pay audits: Conduct regular pay audits across your organization to ensure that bias is not creeping into your pay structure.
- Listen and research: Listen to your employees and research the market. If an employee is saying they are underpaid, it needs to be investigated. Whether it is true or not, doing the research and having the conversation will allow for open and honest interactions with your workforce. If they are correct, bridge the gap. If not, give them the information and explain why they aren't getting

an increase in pay, while also providing plans for potential raises.

Don't assume you don't have a pay equity problem; many companies were surprised to find they had a (sometimes very large) inequity that they didn't realize existed.

Basic Needs: Creative, Safe, and Clean Workplaces

Statements: I have access to creative spaces at work.
I have a safe work environment.
My workplace is clean.

The creative workspace need/statements measures whether employees feel they have access to spaces or resources at work that support creativity and innovation. This may include collaborative workspaces, areas for brainstorming or problem solving, or access to cutting-edge technology and resources.

The workplace safety need/statement assesses whether employees feel their work environment is safe and conducive to their wellbeing. It may include factors such as physical and psychological safety, mental and emotional wellbeing, and appropriate support systems to address any of their concerns.

The clean workplace need/statement measures whether employees feel that their work environment is clean and well-maintained. It may include considerations such as the cleanliness of common areas, the condition of facilities and equipment, and the presence of pests or other hazards.

These are also three separate statements, but I decided to group them together as they are similar in nature. It is important that employees feel that their workspace accommodates their needs. Having a workspace that is creative, safe, and clean is a human need at work. The organization is responsible for providing this for employees in the office and at home.

In an office, things such as clutter, broken equipment, constant noise, and other distracting factors can stunt creativity and, in some cases, be unsafe. In the workplace, psychological safety means feeling safe to share your thoughts, ideas, and emotions without facing ridicule, judgment, or punishment, and these should be a serious consideration for remote and in-person work environments. These factors—whether in person or remote—are not luxuries, but essential needs in any workspace.

Real-Life Examples

I worked on a project with a mining company. The leaders in the company were working on high-level needs, such as vision, purpose, and goal setting. One courageous leader spoke up about the lack of functioning toilets in the field, pointing out that the current ones were in terrible condition. This empathetic leader recognized that the situation was unhygienic and unsafe, and that basic needs had to be met before addressing higher-level goals.

A similar situation occurred with a major hotel chain in the USA, known as one of the best workplaces in the country. In their annual employee survey, staff expressed dissatisfaction with workplace facilities. They noticed that while clients' rooms were being renovated with new furniture and amenities, no improvements were being made to the areas where the employees worked. They wanted to enjoy the same quality as the clients.

The leaders heard their employees' concerns and launched a program called "The Heart of the House," which involved renovating and upgrading the areas where employees got dressed, had their meals, and worked. Their goal was to create a modern, creative, safe, and clean environment where employees could enjoy the same level of quality as their clients.

This program addressed the employees' need for a high-quality workplace environment, and the following year, the organization was voted the number one best workplace in the US by employee votes.

The program demonstrates the importance of workplace creativity, safety, and cleanliness. It is a great example of how listening to and understanding employees' needs can boost engagement and improve workplace culture.

What You Can Do

- Ask yourself if you would like to work in the workplace environment your people are in: Would you send your family members to work there? Is it safe and clean? Fix the basics if you want to show your people are valuable.
- Safety first: Build a culture of safety first with proper policies, training, employee committees,

and champions. Add moments of safety as a culture practice to your team meetings. Be sure your leaders walk the walk.

- Safety includes psychological safety: This is a critical part of the safety umbrella. Extend your safety initiatives to include psychological safety as well. Train your people and equip your leaders to understand this important extension. Make certain that the moments of safety include psychological safety as an equal component to the others.

- A clean workspace shows respect: Have a regular cleaning schedule within the office and provide clear expectations for the cleanliness of common areas to improve employee experience.

- Explore what creativity means for your team/ organization: Ask your employees when and where they feel the most creative at work and promote the practices that allow them to thrive. Understand the two sides of creativity at work: creativity in online meetings, which includes the online facilitation experience of meetings; and on-site creative environments. Is your worksite a great place to gather and brainstorm on the challenges you face?

- Listen to your workforce: If you hear whispers about poor working environments, do something about it.

Basic Need: Wellbeing

Statement: My organization promotes a healthy lifestyle.

This need/statement measures whether employees feel the organization supports and promotes healthy habits and lifestyles. This may include opportunities for physical activity, healthy food options, and resources for managing stress and promoting mental wellbeing.

The pandemic, in many fundamental ways, made employees re-evaluate their priorities, with physical and mental wellbeing becoming a top concern. After witnessing and experiencing illness, exhaustion, and burnout, they now want to work for companies that value their wellbeing and promote a healthy work-life balance in their day-to-day lives.

Case Study

Donovan has been working for a small tech start-up for the past two years. He loves his job and knows that he brings a lot of value to the company with his expertise. However, he feels like something is missing.

Donovan is a very active person; he goes hiking and running on the weekends and tries to stay active during the work week. But long hours spent sitting at a desk often leave him feeling lethargic and unproductive.

He tries to take breaks from his desk to go for a walk or to stretch, but he feels guilty taking time away from his work. No one else in the office goes for walks, and his leaders don't encourage these practices, so eventually Donovan stops as well.

He also struggles with his mental health. He deals with anxiety and stress, and the lack of physical movement during the workday only worsens these challenges. Since his leaders have never emphasized the importance of mental health or conducted wellness checkups with the team, Donovan feels hesitant to discuss his concerns with his boss or coworkers. The company's culture doesn't promote openness about physical and mental health, leaving Donovan feeling stuck.

Over time, Donovan's passion and motivation for his job begin to fade. He still completes his tasks but not at the quality he knows he's capable of. He realizes something needs to change—he is just not sure what.

Shortly after, Donovan runs into a friend who works at another company. His friend mentions all the health and wellness resources available at his workplace, including an onsite gym, free fitness classes, and a stress management program. Donovan realizes that having these resources at work could make a huge difference for his overall wellbeing and productivity. He starts to wonder if he needs to look for a new job that prioritizes both his mental and physical wellbeing.

What You Can Do

- Destigmatize mental health: Equip and encourage your leaders to openly discuss mental health. Many of us have mental health challenges, but this doesn't necessarily impact performance. In fact, many high-performing individuals manage mental health issues. By fostering open conversations and understanding, leaders can help prevent burnout and support long-term team performance.

- Promote physical wellness: Encourage leaders to emphasize the importance of physical wellbeing by normalizing breaks for activity. Leaders should role model behaviors by taking walks during lunch or stretching at their desks. Consider having friendly team challenges that promote physical activity and reward participation. Additionally, provide access to health and wellness resources, such as benefit packages that include counselling, therapy, gym memberships or wellness stipends.

- Role model rest and recovery: Leaders should take their own vacation time and demonstrate what it looks like to truly unplug. By doing so, they encourage employees to take time off and prioritize rest and recovery.

- Create white space on your calendars and video call-free days: "Zoom fatigue" is real. Consider making video optional or hosting video-free meetings. Many organizations are also declaring dedicated meeting-free time, like "No Meeting Mondays," or blocking off every Wednesday afternoon for the entire organization. These dedicated breaks help employees recharge and enhance productivity.

- Train leaders to develop coaching skills: Leaders who know how to coach are better equipped to support their employees during challenging situations. They can ask insightful questions, help set clear goals, and work through underlying issues more effectively.

- Help leaders develop emotional intelligence: Knowing how to regulate their own emotions and steer the emotions of those around them towards beneficial results is considered a key leadership skill.

Basic Need: Employee Consideration

Statement: Policies, practices, and procedures are derived from employee needs.

This need/statement assesses whether employees feel the policies, practices, and procedures of the organization are designed with their needs and wellbeing in mind. This may include employee surveys, pulse surveys, employee consultations, listening circles, flexible work arrangements, and processes for addressing employee concerns or feedback.

Employees desire to feel acknowledged, appreciated, and understood. When an organization's policies demonstrate that it recognizes the significance of its employees and their contributions to the success of the company, employees are more likely to be motivated and invested in their work.

Case Study

Jasmine has been working as a consultant at the same company for three years and is content with her job and her relationships with colleagues. She appreciates the opportunities for professional growth and the positive work culture at the organization. However, things start to change when the company takes on an important project.

During a meeting with senior leaders, Jasmine and her coworkers are informed of the importance of the project for the company's growth. At first, Jasmine appreciates the open communication, but as the project progresses, she begins to notice a shift in expectations. Deadlines tighten, the workload intensifies, and long hours—including weekends— become the norm. Email communication outside of work hours also increases.

Initially, Jasmine is willing to check her email after hours to stay on top of things, but as time goes on, the expectation becomes more intense. One evening, Jasmine receives an urgent email after leaving work and is unable to respond until the next morning. Her manager questions her about the delay, and Jasmine realizes that the expectation to check her email after hours has become an unspoken rule. It is clear that if emails are left unanswered, it causes delays for the project.

Jasmine is frustrated with these unrealistic expectations and struggles to maintain a healthy work-life balance. She wants the company to do well and grow, but she begins to feel overwhelmed and exhausted. Her colleagues feel the same way, but no one speaks up about it. They assume that it is a temporary sacrifice to ensure the success of the project.

As the project comes to an end, Jasmine and her colleagues approach their manager to express their concerns. They explain how the unrealistic expectations have impacted their mental health. They suggest the company consider their workload and wellbeing when taking on large projects in the future. Unfortunately, their leader justifies the excessive demand, saying that the project was crucial for the company's growth.

Realizing that the company values profit over its employees, Jasmine makes the difficult decision to leave the organization, followed by many of her coworkers who feel the same way.

What You Can Do

- Revisit your policies and procedures: Evaluate and review your policies and procedures to see whether they set any unrealistic expectations for your employees. Assess your organization's values and culture and whether different perspectives, contexts, and life circumstances have been considered. Your policies should promote employees, and not set up barriers for them.
- Build a culture of consultation: When the company is going through change or development, consider how it affects the employees, and ask them. Surveys, pulse checks or town halls are a great way to get the general feeling or consensus of your workforce without asking too much of them. Provide employees with the opportunity to give feedback, and act on it. Many employees will

give feedback when they feel it is necessary, but others will not speak up and say what they really think. Once feedback is given, it is important to act on it. Implementation is a crucial part of making real organizational change, and this is an essential component of the Culture-Actualization Index© process. We emphasize the importance of creating a culture action plan and regularly revising and evaluating it. Data is only the first step of the process, and if no action is taken based on the findings, it may lead to a negative cycle of inactivity and a reduced sense of employee consideration.

- Train your leaders on human-centered thinking and how to engage in Leading with Culture©. With these mindsets, they will develop better listening and observing skills and will be equipped to build culture practices and team rituals that stem from their teams' needs.

Basic Need: Inclusivity

Statement: My organization listens to diverse ideas.

This need/statement measures whether employees feel their organization values and actively seeks out diverse perspectives and ideas. This may include aspects such as employee and pulse surveys, townhalls where leaders genuinely answer questions, leadership reach outs, leaders spending time in the field, inclusivity and diversity training, and support for employees from underrepresented groups.

It's encouraging that inclusion is now receiving greater focus and attention in both the corporate world and society at large. In our initial qualitative research, inclusivity was considered a psychological need. However, after conducting quantitative research, we learned that inclusivity had evolved into a basic need. This speaks to the fact that inclusivity is a necessity in the workplace! The reality is inclusion is a prerequisite for building a high-performing, people-focused organization. If we can't solve this challenge, we won't reach our full potential.

As a response, many organizations have formed diversity and inclusion committees, developed DEI strategies, implemented ways to measure progress (such as surveys), and taken employees through bias training. Yet, managers are struggling with the next step. In fact, a common criticism of DEI programs is that they are all talk with no action. So then, what do we do about it?

Inclusion is a complex topic and can't be reduced to one approach. The starting point to inclusion is ensuring diverse representation across the organization. Diversity, whether demographic or cognitive, is a prerequisite for inclusion. It involves bringing together people with different backgrounds, personalities, learning styles, and a host of other variables.

The people leading inclusion efforts should be those who have a personal stake in it—the underrepresented groups. There are many experts in this space that can help organizations create truly transformative inclusion policies. Based on my personal experience, inclusivity increases when managers are trained to become coaches. This is because it helps managers develop the skill to ask questions from a non-judgmental and curious place, fostering belief in people's potential.

Case Study

At a software development company, a team of programmers works long hours, often staying late to meet tight deadlines. Ali, a member of this team, enjoys the work but finds the environment far from inclusive.

There is an obvious "in" group within the team—colleagues who socialize after work and collaborate closely on projects. It is obvious who belongs to this group and who doesn't.

Ali often finds himself excluded from key meetings and conversations he feels are important, but he's unsure how to approach the situation and bridge the gap. When he raises the issue with his manager, he is told that he isn't a "team player" and that he needs to work harder to fit in.

Despite his efforts, Ali feels increasingly isolated at work. He notices that other team members who are not part of the "in" group also struggle to be heard and included. Ali tries to connect with them to create a sense of community but is met with disengagement and discouragement. Ali realizes that the problem is the team culture; it is toxic and affects everyone's productivity and wellbeing.

Along with a few colleagues, Ali speaks up and advocates for a more inclusive workplace, believing that if everyone felt included, the team would work more effectively and enjoy their day-to-day.

However, their efforts are met with resistance and hostility from the "in" group who accuse them of being "oversensitive" and "causing drama" in the workplace.

Eventually, Ali and several others leave the company, unable to continue working in such an unwelcoming environment. The company faces high turnover and low morale, yet the managers remain blind to the root cause of the problem.

What You Can Do

- Improve your DEI plan: Consult with DEI experts to ensure the plan you have is meaningful and effective. We are ready to help on this topic with our world-renowned experts in this field.
- Build an inclusive culture: Recognize that taking your employees through online DEI training alone is not enough Building an effective DEI program requires a systematic approach that integrates inclusivity into your organizational culture.
- Follow through with action: Make sure you act on your DEI commitments and regularly check-in to ensure these actions are delivering the desired results.
- Encourage practices that build your team: Make coaching competencies a core part of leadership, including at the C-suite level. Ensure employees receive regular feedback and coaching, with leaders who maintain curiosity and a growth mindset.

- Implement shadow coaching: Consider using shadow coaching, where a DEI-trained coach observes leaders in action during meetings. This provides valuable insights into how leaders are role-modeling DEI through their language and behavior.

Basic Need: Networking Opportunities

Statement: My organization provides networking opportunities.

This need/statement assesses whether employees feel they have opportunities to connect and build relationships with others within and outside of the organization. This may include access to and encouragement to attend networking events, professional development opportunities, and mentorship programs.

Just like inclusivity, in our initial qualitative research, networking was considered a psychological need. After our quantitative research, we learned that networking had evolved into a basic need. The opportunity to connect with others appears to be essential for a positive employee experience and healthy workplace culture.

Networking allows employees to gain stronger connections with their colleagues and other professionals working in the industry. This helps them stay up to date with the latest trends, knowledge, and information in their industry.

Networking can also help employees build their personal brand and facilitate their career development by establishing relationships with high level professionals in their workplace. It can lead to increased collaboration, partnerships, and connection, and is related to the psychological needs of camaraderie and positive interactions, as well as any other need that requires connection.

Case Study

Stefan has been working in the sales department of his organization for just over a year. While he enjoys his work, he feels disconnected from the company and sees few opportunities for professional growth. He finds it challenging to build relationships with colleagues and believes that this is hindering his career advancement.

Recently, the company launched an internal networking program. At first, Stefan hesitates to attend, worried that his lack of strong connections will make the event awkward or uncomfortable. However, after hearing about an upcoming staff lunch and receiving some encouragement from his leader, he decides to give it a try.

To his surprise, the event is very welcoming and inclusive. The leader introduces an icebreaker activity that helps everyone feel at ease, and Stefan has the chance to meet coworkers he didn't know before. He even makes plans with a couple of coworkers to go out on a Friday evening. He also has a meaningful conversation with his leader, leaving him excited about potential future opportunities.

Encouraged by this positive experience, Stefan begins attending more events, such as team building activities, mentorship sessions, peer programs, and lunch-and-learns.

He starts building strong connections within the organization and stands out amongst his colleagues. With the company's support in providing networking opportunities, Stefan's employee experience improves significantly.

A few months later, Stefan's leader recommends him for a promotion, and he is thrilled about the recognition. Looking back, he wishes he had participated in these events sooner, but he is grateful for the chance to connect with others while also advancing his career and professional development.

What You Can Do

- Prioritize networking: Provide opportunities for employes to network both within and outside the organization.
- Make new employees feel welcome at events: Networking can be intimidating, especially for new or introverted employees. To make internal events more inclusive, use conversation prompts, lead ice breakers, and create a welcoming atmosphere. Remember that many company events cater to extraverts, so consider incorporating more introvert-friendly activities, reflection time, and structured ways for people to get to know each other.
- Find simple and effective ways to maintain relationships: It can be challenging to nurture connections with coworkers amidst busy schedules. To keep networking manageable, offer regular, low-key team lunches to bring people together without overwhelming them.

- Clarify your internal communication channels: Develop meeting and culture practices that help participants connect and get to know each other better.
- Promote collaboration: Encourage employees to dedicate some of their work time for task forces or cross-departmental projects, allowing them to collaborate and build relationships across the organization.

In this chapter, I reviewed the research findings on thirteen basic needs that employees have in today's workforce. Topics like inclusion, wellbeing, networking, and creativity at work, which were once considered higher-level needs, have now become basic needs, which makes many leaders and organizations struggle to understand what they are not doing. There is an increased expectation on organizations to help employees manage their wellbeing or have seamless onboarding experiences. If these needs are not met, employees don't hesitate to find work elsewhere.

CHAPTER 4

Decoding the Hierarchy of Needs at Work: Psychological Needs

The psychological needs identified in our research changed drastically after analyzing our most recent quantitative data. Previously, in first round of our research (see Appendix), there were five main categories of psychological needs: social connections, inclusion, collaboration, learning and development (L&D), and the trio of recognition-appreciation-celebration. After the second round of research, inclusion emerged as a basic need. Our initial observation that L&D built self-esteem and was considered a psychological need turned out to be incorrect.

The L&D statements were found to be basic needs, closely tied to onboarding. Initially, L&D expectations revolved around formal programs and training events. However, the focus has shifted to proper onboarding and thorough training on tools, equipment, software, and job expectations.

Our research also revealed that employees expect to learn directly from their leaders, and that proper onboarding and mentoring from their leader is considered the most important form of L&D an organization can offer. Other statements moved up into the growth needs, where the leader is now expected to coach, mentor, and give feedback.

Another interesting change in this category was that appreciation and recognition dropped off the culture-actualization statements entirely. Companies spend millions of dollars on recognition programs, but our research suggests we reconsider these investments.

People no longer seem to value traditional forms of recognition, like being named employee of the month. Instead, they appreciate when their leaders and colleagues genuinely know them, understand their preferences, and recognize their accomplishments in meaningful ways. It's not about copy-pasted thank-you emails or generic appreciation programs—it's about leaders showing genuine respect and trust.

Our current research suggests that organizations may not need to spend as much on recognition programs and online training; instead, the focus should be on training leaders to become effective coaches and mentors who can meet their employees' needs.

The Culture-Actualization Index© reveals that psychological needs are deeply tied to employees' relationship with their colleagues and peers. We must help employees understand their role in creating good corporate citizenship and building a healthy community, because they add so much to the human experience at work.

Psychological Needs: Camaraderie and Positive Interactions

Statements: There is a sense of friendship at work.

I like the people I interact with at work.

The camaraderie need/statement measures whether employees feel a sense of camaraderie and positive interpersonal relationships with their coworkers. This can include supportive and respectful interactions, a feeling of community and opportunities for socializing outside of work.

The positive interactions need/statement measures whether employees feel they have supportive and positive relationships with their coworkers. It can include mutual respect, helpfulness, and teamwork.

Again, I grouped these processes together because of their similarities. Many people struggle with the idea of friendship in the workplace. Do we need to be friends at work?

Throughout our research, our understanding has evolved to this: employees don't have to become best friends, but a sense of friendliness and friendship in the workplace goes a long way. For example, Gallup's Q12 Engagement Survey explicitly asked employees if they have a best friend at work. As much as this can be helpful for engagement, having best friends in the workplace can be a double-edged sword. If one's best friend at work leaves, how does the remaining person feel?

Strong friendships at work can sometimes lead to cliques or different alliances within teams. I am not condemning having best friends at work—after all, having one made my own work experience so much more enjoyable. What I am trying to highlight is that, from a cultural perspective, it's not the presence of a best friend that improves workplace quality. Instead, it's about fostering a friendly, inclusive culture in the workplace where positive interactions and a sense of belonging thrive

Traditionally, people connected in the office. Informal "water cooler" chats, team potlucks, or formally organized events were all hallmarks of office life. "Friends" fans may also remember the episode where Rachel takes up smoking because she wanted to be included in the decisions made during cigarette breaks!

Virtual water coolers, remote conferences, social Slack or similar channels, and the like can all help create a connected atmosphere in the modern workplace. The hybrid future will be particularly challenging for fostering social connections across work locations. Again, it's important to watch out for virtual fatigue, as too many Zoom meetings quickly become toxic. Our need for positive interactions is related to the concept of positive climate in culture studies: the foundation of a healthy climate is healthy interactions.

However, this doesn't mean avoiding the negative. Rather, it emphasizes the importance of knowing how to deal with difficult or negative conversations. Similarly, emotional intelligence is not just about bringing raw emotions or emotionality to work; EQ is also about building the right skillsets to understand emotions and learn from emotions in a healthy way. Positive interactions in the workplace include learning how to deal with negative situations in a more constructive and mature way.

Culture practices that help build trust and a shared language have an important role in building these positive interactions. Our Leading with Culture© program trains people managers on how to develop these kinds of culture practices.

Workplace arrangements in the post-Covid-19 era are becoming increasingly flexible to meet the evolving needs of employees. These changes are also sparking new research and discussions, raising questions that hadn't been considered before—such as the fundamental yet elusive issue of how many days in the office are ideal for hybrid work. How do fully remote organizations build belonging?

Today, as research results are improving, many findings suggest that the optimal balance for hybrid work is around three days per week in the office. Gallup's Hybrid Work Indicators study (2023) shows that engagement peaks at two and three days per week in the office for both collaborative workers (those who need to work closely with others) and asynchronous workers (those who can work independently of common hours).

The best suggestion we have for this topic is to understand your employees' needs and the national/ regional culture you operate within, while also considering the competitiveness of the talent market. Gathering firsthand evidence, talking to employees, or surveying employees to understand their needs demonstrates employee-centeredness and inclusion.

It is important to understand that you can't simply survey your employees on their preferences and then disregard their input. There are numerous stories of CEOs reviewing employee survey results only to go in a completely different direction. This creates a downward spiral of losing trust and sends a clear message: "We don't care about you; this machine needs to move forward with or without you." We can easily predict the negative reaction to such a tone-deaf corporate philosophy.

Organizations must be intentional about how and where they host meetings and events, always mindful of whom they include and exclude. Careful consideration of employee preferences and schedules is essential for successfully fostering connection.

Another issue to watch closely is favoritism toward employees who are more frequently in the office versus those who do not or cannot come in as often. The sub-cultures or micro cultures that form between in-office and remote workers are increasingly becoming a focus of DEI programs as well.

To highlight once more, the needs at different levels are all interrelated. We feel multiple needs at any given time, and we prioritize them based on culture and context. Camaraderie, positive interactions, and belonging have parallels with inclusion, networking in the organization, on-boarding, and job security, as well as the leader's role modeling of inclusive decision making, working collaboratively and cohesively with the team and with other leaders.

Case Study

A design team within a large organization recently experienced significant changes, including the addition of a new manager and four new hires. The team already had three seasoned employees, two of whom had formed a close friendship and alliance.

The onboarding process for the new employees goes very well; everyone is supportive and optimistic about the restructuring of the team. However, the new hires soon start to notice passive-aggressive comments and subtle hostile disagreement between the two allied seasoned employees and the third, more isolated seasoned employee.

This creates a power dynamic that leaves the new hires feeling pressured to choose sides. Unaware of the underlying tension, the new manager—who relies heavily on the three seasoned employees—fails to notice the hostility.

As the new hires confide in one another, they express feelings of exclusion and confusion about why there is so much unnecessary conflict. The environment becomes toxic, stifling positive interactions and leaving the new employees feeling overwhelmed. Eventually, they leave the organization due to the negative dynamic.

What You Can Do

- Address toxicity in the workplace: Train your leaders, managers, and employees to become aware of and understand their role in creating a safe and inclusive workplace environment. Give your employees the tools and the language to call out and challenge toxic behaviors. When there is a power dynamic at play, employees may feel trapped and uncomfortable directly confronting their colleague. Make sure to include resources as well as structures for reporting toxic or other inappropriate behavior so employees feel safe speaking up.

- Consider employee preferences: Survey your employees to determine social connection preferences, and tailor activities accordingly. Not everyone enjoys social hours, so create opportunities that reflect diverse needs

- Make it relevant: Develop culture practices such as check-in circles to personalize meeting time.

- Keep it engaging: Ensure that events in the office are meaningful and enticing. Consider holding bigger events a few times a year and subsidizing travel to encourage participation.

- Foster collaboration: Put the control back in your employees' hands by creating a social committee that helps steer the direction. Encourage social committees to activate smaller interest groups, not just large events.

- Activity is key: Stay consistent and maintain engagement with social channels and remote tools. Reward employees for their participation to keep the momentum going.

Psychological Need: Organizational Belonging

Statement: I feel like I belong at my organization.

This need/statement assesses whether employees feel a sense of belonging and acceptance within their organization. It may include factors such as alignment with company values and culture, support from coworkers and leadership, and opportunities for integration and involvement in the company.

Belonging is a complex and often misunderstood topic. Our research shows that it primarily revolves around a sense of acceptance an employee feels – particularly with their colleagues and the workplace community.

This concept is an extension of the onboarding process, which should prioritize welcoming employees and ensuring they feel included in the workplace community. Effective onboarding begins by addressing basic needs and fostering camaraderie to create a welcoming environment and a sense of belonging.

Belonging is not created with a few team building activities like throwing balls or climbing ropes. While these can be fun, they rarely lead to meaningful changes in team dynamics.

Authentic belonging comes from true connections, from genuine relationships and trust. For example, in our North Star Coaching© workshop, individuals work on identifying their personal North Stars, followed by the team collaborating on a shared North Star. This connection of the personal and the team creates a deeper connection and acknowledgement of the individual and the team dynamics.

Ongoing team coaching helps teams talk about the "elephants in the room" in a constructive way, allowing them to move forward to reach their collective potential.

Case Study

Cameron is new to an organization. As a hybrid worker, the first few weeks of their transition period have been difficult. Although their onboarding process was thorough, they are beginning to realize that the company culture focuses heavily on results and performance and does not prioritize relationship-building or connection.

Cameron is no stranger to hard work and is happy to dedicate their working hours to assigned tasks—that's what they were hired to do. However, they can't help but feel like something is missing.

In the first virtual meeting they attend on one of their work-from-home days, Cameron is quickly introduced to the team by their leader: "Hi everyone, this is Cameron." The leader then immediately jumps into work and delegating tasks.

Cameron isn't given an opportunity to speak, introduce themselves, or meet the other team members, which they think is a bit odd. Cameron figures this is due to the meeting agenda being heavy and the pressing tasks at hand, so they don't dwell on it.

In the office, coworkers take breaks outside of the office and spend the majority of their time in their cubicles. While Cameron has had some conversations with their colleagues, they are often interrupted by meetings or cut short by heavy workloads and short timelines.

In Cameron's previous positions at different organizations, leaders always started the meetings with check-ins, asking their team how their weekend was or simply how they are doing. As weeks go by, Cameron notices this is not the norm at their new organization; they seldom do check-ins or ask each other about their lives. Another new hire comes into a meeting and gets the same quick introduction that Cameron did. Also, in the first few months of Cameron's employment, there are no social activities for employees to connect with one another.

Cameron enjoys the work they are doing, but doesn't feel like anyone at the organization, especially their leaders, knows them on a personal level. They don't realize it at first, but it begins to take a toll on them. They feel like a cog in the machine, replaceable and disposable. Cameron is valuable in their own unique way, but the organization has not fostered their connection to coworkers or a sense of community, which makes Cameron feel like they don't belong.

What You Can Do

- Foster engagement: Encourage employee involvement while acknowledging different personalities and preferences for connecting. Incentivizing employees to take part of social events and group discussions and rewarding them for participating is a great tactic to accommodate the belonging needs of your extroverted workforce. Consider your introverted workers too; they may feel less connected and included if they are frequently overshadowed by their extroverted colleagues in meetings. To foster a greater sense of belonging, it can be helpful to provide them with a safe and supportive space to express their thoughts and ideas without the pressure of competing with more outgoing individuals in the room.

- Show interest in how they're doing: For new remote and hybrid employees, have frequent check-ins about their integration into the employee culture. Don't test them on what they know or who they have connected with, but genuinely ask them how they feel like they belong in the organization.

- Be mindful of the language you use: Referring to individuals as "team members" rather than "employees" can foster a greater sense of belonging within the organization. This small shift may seem trivial, but language matters. The words you choose can impact both the need for organizational belonging and inclusion of your team members. Inclusive language plays a big role in a positive workplace culture. For example, avoid saying "my" team instead of "our" team—leaders don't own the team, they're part of it. Eliminating any kind of language that reflects prejudice, stereotypes, or discrimination will help prevent discomfort and marginalization. Feeling accepted into a workplace is a vital part of the employee experience, and using mindful, inclusive language is a responsibility shared by everyone in the workplace.

In this chapter, I reviewed the research findings on psychological needs at work. Psychological needs were initially inspired by the belonging, love, and esteem levels of Maslow's Hierarchy of Needs. Our initial conceptual framework, based on qualitative research, contained more items/needs. As we conducted the quantitative research, we were surprised to find that many of the needs were better categorized as basic or growth needs. Ultimately, the psychological needs were distilled into three clear themes: belonging, camaraderie, and positive interactions.

The psychological needs ended up being primarily based on our relationship with other employees, emphasizing the importance of community in the workplace. This highlights our duty to be non-toxic colleagues, and our responsibility to build positive climates or environments at work where we can all enjoy working together. In the next chapter, I will follow the same structure and discuss the ten growth needs our research revealed.

CHAPTER 5

Decoding the Hierarchy of Needs at Work: Growth Needs

According to our research, the growth needs of employees are closely tied to their relationship with their leaders. The leader plays a critical role in enabling employee growth, development, and actualization.

This is consistent with the saying that people join organizations but leave managers, as leaders have the power to make or break the employee experience. Creating a culture of actualization is heavily influenced by leaders' role modeling behaviors. Our research showed that employees are more interested in whether their leaders genuinely live the organization's purpose than in the organization's North Star or purpose itself.

Employees seek leaders who role model values, broadcast the purpose of the organization, have clear goals, and demonstrate cohesive leadership. Employees also want inclusive leaders who involve them in decision-making. The study highlights the importance of coaching, mentoring, cultivating trust, and providing genuine feedback in developing leaders. To measure progress in developing leaders, evaluating growth needs and creating a leadership index can be helpful.

Growth Needs: Purpose Broadcasting and Clear Goal Setting

Statements: My leader communicates the organization's purpose with employees.

My leader sets clear goals and objectives.

The purpose broadcasting need/statement assesses whether employees feel their leaders effectively communicate the purpose and goals of the organization and whether they feel a sense of alignment with those goals. This may include clear and regular communication, opportunities for input and feedback, and a shared understanding of the company's direction.

The clear goal setting need/statement assesses whether employees feel their leaders set clear and measurable goals and objectives for the team or organization and whether they provide the necessary support and resources to achieve those goals. This may include giving regular progress reviews, providing feedback and guidance, and aligning goals with the overall direction of the company.

Purpose broadcasting is a common oversight in many organizations. While all organizations have a purpose, it is not always well-defined, articulated, or effectively implemented. Both employees and customers desire a purpose that is inspiring and meaningful, and that is embodied by leaders.

In addition, employees want clear and tangible individual goals that are aligned with the company's purpose. This alignment, along with clearly communicated expectations, can significantly increase their motivation to produce high-quality work.

Case Study

Mina is the social media manager at her organization. She recently returned to in-person work following the Covid-19 pandemic and is happy to be back in the office. However, this transition has caused a lapse in communication with her manager, who is also adjusting to being back. This new dynamic is taking longer for both of them to adapt to than expected, which worries Mina.

In the past, Mina has struggled with her manager's delayed communication, and she hopes this transition period doesn't set her even farther back.

During a meeting, she notices a shift in her colleagues' language regarding the organization's strategy. While the company initially focused on a business-to-consumer (B2C) marketing approach, her coworkers now discuss a business-to-business (B2B) strategy on the services side of the organization. They also mention new organizational goals that Mina hadn't been informed about.

As the social media manager, Mina is surprised and frustrated that she wasn't briefed on such a significant change. Embarrassed, she admits during the meeting that she had not been informed about the new strategy, and as the leader of the social media team, she feels like she let them down.

Mina suspects this is due to her manager's communication lapse. While she understands it's a transition period for both, she feels a major change like this should not go unmentioned, regardless of the circumstances. Mina requests a meeting with her manager to discuss the issue.

She respectfully expresses her frustration, explaining what happened in the meeting and asking for improved communication moving forward. Her manager acknowledges the mistake, apologizes for the oversight, and admits that they should have delivered this information directly to Mina.

They agree that it's critical for Mina to stay updated on the company's strategy and do not attribute the communication breakdown to the transition. The manager explains they had assumed Mina would learn about the strategy through colleagues or in meetings, but they recognize this approach was ineffective. They commit to better communication going forward.

The manager's sincere apology, along with their subsequent actions, leads to much better communication. They now check in regularly to align on goals and strategy. Not only does Mina have a clear understanding of the new direction, but she also feels a stronger dynamic with her manager for giving and receiving feedback.

What You Can Do

- Broadcast your purpose and goals: Ensure the onboarding process articulates the organization's purpose. During onboarding and training, it's essential that employees understand both their individual roles and the broader objectives the organization is striving to achieve.

- Prioritize being a united company: Routinely check-in with employees to align goals and mindsets. In the post-Covid-19 era, companies and organizations are adapting and changing quickly. This can mean changes in strategy, values, and purpose. To remain aligned, regular check-ins are crucial.

- Encourage constructive communication: Provide opportunities for input and feedback for both leaders and employees. Without feedback, leaders may be unaware if they are effectively articulating the company's purpose. Providing employees with a chance to share their thoughts and personally articulate their perception of the organization's purpose can facilitate better alignment of goals and a more meaningful experience for everyone involved.

Growth Needs: Values Role Modeling and Leadership Role Modeling

Statements: My leader role models our organization's values.

My leader is a good role model.

The values role modeling need/statement measures whether employees feel their leaders embody and model the values and behaviors that are important to the organization. This may include behaviors that demonstrate integrity, fairness, and accountability.

The leadership role modeling need/statement assesses whether employees feel their leader is a good role model, exhibiting leadership in the sense of focusing on others, such as employees and clients, more than on themselves.

Simply stating that the organization is inclusive or welcoming is not enough; leaders must actively demonstrate these values through their actions. When leaders model these behaviors consistently, employees are more likely to adopt them and incorporate them into their own actions and decisions. When leaders embody the values and behaviors of the organization, it fosters a sense of belonging and loyalty among employees, which can lead to higher engagement and retention rates.

Case Study

Ravi recently started as an environmental consultant at a green energy company. The company has a clear mission; to make green energy mainstream and sustainability an everyday practice. Passionate about environmental issues, Ravi is eager to contribute to making a difference. He quickly immerses himself in the company's culture, embodying its values and showing his commitment to sustainability.

Unfortunately, Ravi quickly notices that his manager isn't acting in accordance with the company's values. He frequently leaves his computer and office lights on overnight, wastes excessive paper by printing unnecessary documents, and doesn't dispose of or recycle items properly.

This disappoints Ravi, causing him to lose some faith in the company. If his manager isn't modeling sustainability, how can they expect others to follow suit? Ravi feels conflicted. While he's developed a relationship with his manager, there isn't enough trust yet to approach him directly about the issue. Instead, Ravi brings his concerns to a higher-level manager he met during his onboarding. They listen attentively, thank him for raising the issue, and assure him it will be addressed.

In the following weeks, Ravi notices positive changes in his manager's behavior. Lights are no longer left on, garbage and recycling bins now have clearer labels and instructions, and one day, Ravi even saw his manager biking to work.

Ravi appreciates that his manager is now role modeling the values of the company and leading by example. His manager even organizes a lunch to share what he's doing in his everyday life to promote sustainability, while also acknowledging that he has faltered with his efforts in the past. This inspires Ravi to deepen his own commitment to sustainability and restores his passion and belief in the company's mission.

What You Can Do

- Define leadership behaviors clearly: Further clarify how the values are lived out and how they aren't. These behaviors must be observable and tangible, not just abstract concepts. For example, "We are inclusive in how we work" is a concept. "We show inclusion by asking, listening, and thinking about how we hear" is observable.

- Train your leaders on Leading with Culture©: Help them better understand the importance of role modeling at work.
- Maintain accountability: Build culture practices that teach all leaders and employees how to respectfully call out behaviors that don't align with the company's values. Role modeling isn't just about what leaders do—it's also about what they don't do or what they permit to happen.
- Seek external feedback: Bring in on-the-job coaching, also called shadow coaching or behavioral coaching, where a trained coach accompanies leaders to observe meetings and conversations, and then provides feedback to the manager.
- Measure your culture: Use the Culture-Actualization Index©, as a key performance indicator, demonstrating your organization's commitment to culture.

Growth Needs: Cohesiveness and Inclusive Decision-Making

Statements: My leader has a productive working relationship with upper management.

My leader encourages employees to participate in decision-making.

The cohesiveness need/statement measures whether employees feel their leader has a productive and positive working relationship with other leaders. This may involve a clear, organization-wide strategy that all leaders understand and share, supported by a unified purpose, aligned goals, and effective communication. This also includes transparency, collaboration, shared decision-making and demonstrated alignment.

The inclusive decision-making need/statement assesses whether employees feel their leader encourages and values their participation in decision-making and problem-solving. This may include soliciting input and feedback, considering different perspectives, and providing opportunities for employees to take on leadership roles.

Many organizations need to make significant improvements in fostering cohesiveness. Our research indicates that leaders struggle to operate as a cohesive team. Instead, many, including executive leaders, primarily identify and feel aligned only with their own department and fail to view their peers as part of the cohesive team.

During meetings, executive leaders tend to represent their department instead of collaborating with their peers to overcome obstacles. This behavior often results in individual siloes, disconnection, and self-interest rather than collective progress.

This issue is directly linked to inclusive decision-making. When decisions are made without consulting those affected, it can leave individuals feeling undervalued, like mere cogs in the machine. That is why it is crucial to be inclusive when making decisions.

While leaders may think they know what's best for their team, ignoring their input can signal that their opinions are not valued, negatively affecting the overall employee experience.

Cohesion and inclusion are indicators that employees prefer leaders who work collaboratively with others. Just as children can sense when their parents are fighting, employees can detect when leaders aren't getting along. When leaders fail to work together, they hinder the organization's ability to achieve its full potential.

Case Study

Dakota works in client recruitment at her organization. Her team leader has expressed frustration with upper management, citing stress caused by a high-ranking individual. Despite their team's strong performance, they've been told upper management is dissatisfied and that changes may be coming.

A few weeks later, Dakota's manager sends her team a brief outlining a new client recruitment strategy, which requires them to communicate solely by phone. The brief claims that this will improve client communication and increase sales.

Dakota feels overwhelmed and confused by the sudden change. She doesn't have phone numbers for many of her clients and worries that calling those she has only ever communicated with by email could seem intrusive and confusing.

Furthermore, she has achieved strong results in recent months using email as the standard procedure and doesn't understand the need to switch to exclusively phone communication.

When Dakota voices her concerns to her manager, she's told that the decision came from upper management and is out of her manager's control. This leaves her feeling frustrated and unmotivated.

Despite her reservations, Dakota begins implementing the new strategy and finds that most of her calls go unanswered and client interest drops. It's only when her leader recognizes the drop in client interest that she acknowledges Dakota was right, apologizes for not consulting her before accepting the change, and promises to bring the issue to upper management for review.

Soon after, the original strategy is reinstated, and Dakota's sales begin to increase again. However, she remains disappointed by the lack of communication and decision-making that affected her workflow. She feels frustrated that her manager did not consult her before making such a significant change and discouraged by the disconnect between upper management and her team leader.

What You Can Do

- Understand the importance of community within an organization: Consider an organization-wide strategy to align departments under shared goals and a unified purpose.
- Encourage unity and teamwork: Employ regular executive team coaching with a focus on alignment and collaboration. Executives role modeling culture and focusing on the internal and external culture practices are what set the tone for the rest of the employees within the company culture.
- Remove hierarchical processes: Eliminate policies or procedures that promote competition

or departmental superiority, especially at the executive level.

- Foster collaboration and feedback: Ask employees what they think about a potential decision or how it might affect them. Simple questions go a long way.

Growth Needs: Coaching, Mentoring, and Constructive Feedback

Statements: My leader is a great coach.

My leader is a great mentor.

My leader provides feedback in a positive manner.

The coaching role need/statement measures whether employees feel their leader serves as a coach, providing guidance and support to help them improve their performance and achieve their goals. This may include regular coaching conversations, spaces for reflective dialogue, open-ended questions, active listening, and feedback that creates awareness, ownership, accountability, empowerment, and personal responsibility.

The mentoring need/statement measures whether employees feel their leader serves as a mentor, providing guidance and support for their professional development. This may include offering advice and feedback, helping to set and achieve career goals, sharing life experiences in the right moments, and passing over valuable life lessons.

The constructive feedback need/statement measures whether employees feel they receive timely and constructive feedback from their leader. This may include regular check-ins, specific and actionable recommendations for improvement, and a focus on strengths and areas for growth. This element goes hand in hand with coaching and mentoring. There is increasing evidence of the value of building a coaching culture. According to the International Coaching Federation's 2019 Coaching Cultures research, organizations with strong coaching cultures are nearly twice as likely to be high-performing compared to those without one.

Gallup's 2019 book *It's The Manager* advises that if leaders must prioritize one action, it should be teaching their managers coaching skills. Google's Project Oxygen researched the great Google managers' behaviors and identified that effective coaching was the foundational behavior upon which all other positive behaviors were built.

A coaching culture reflects a workplace that takes a holistic approach to coaching by training leaders in coaching skills, developing internal coaching programs, and strategically utilizing external coaches. Currently, most coaching efforts consist of a single, one-off coach selection for an individual leader. I have led several culture transformation coaching projects where, as team of coaches, we supported forty to one hundred leaders, from C-level to directors, over a six-to-twelve-month period. These projects integrated annual culture surveys with facilitated action plans, pulse surveys, culture consulting, training programs, team coaching, and 1:1 coaching sessions.

The increasing body of evidence on coaching and ROI studies show the impact of coaching in organizations.

While Fortune 500 companies are reevaluating their leadership competencies through a coaching lens, they are also developing strategies that define the roles of external coaches, internal coaches, and leaders as coaches. To be clear, leadership development without coaching is merely entertainment. Many leaders learn about topics and concepts, yet do not change their mindset, habits, or behaviors.

Having coaching as an integral part of a manager's role is critical to reaching self-actualization. As organizations recognize this, there's a growing trend to include coaching programs in the overall budget, turning them into a permanent commitment rather than a one-time initiative.

I want to highlight the importance of balancing coaching and mentorship. When viewed as roles (coach or mentor), they serve different purposes and meet distinct needs. However, when seen as skills (coaching skills, mentoring skills), there is significant overlap. As coaching gains popularity, I want to ensure we don't forget the value and importance of good mentorship. Our research reveals that statements on mentorship and coaching have a 99% identical impact on the overall index, and both are essential. So, as the importance of coaching is rising, we need to be sure that mentorship skills and programs are equally prioritized.

I have been both a coach and a mentor in my life, and the impact of mentors is profound. I can recall several leaders who mentored me throughout my professional career, and I still remember how they affected me.

Leaders who act as mentors show a commitment to employee success. That creates trust, dedication, and a positive influence in the workplace. I found it most effective to train leaders and managers in both coaching and mentorship skills, along with the ability to navigate between them and leverage their shared skills when needed.

I think great mentors use a lot of coaching skills. This is why we created the program Leader as a Coach and Mentor© at Maslow Research Center, which combines both skillsets. Most training programs for coaches either focus on building a coaching practice, being an external coach, or simply training leaders on coaching skills. Our approach equips leaders with both coaching and mentorship competencies, teaching them when and how to apply each, and even how to blend these approaches in various situations.

Feedback is a core competency in both coaching and mentorship. In many cases, bottlenecks in the workplace occur due to a lack of timely feedback. When employees are waiting for feedback from their leader, they can become frustrated or stuck, which hinders progress. Clear expectations regarding the timeline and type of feedback should be set to avoid such issues. The quality of feedback is equally important, as poorly formulated or insufficient thoughts can lead to misunderstandings about its purpose or leave employees confused about how to interpret it.

We encourage organizations to develop a holistic coaching and mentorship strategy that aligns with their learning and development (L&D), talent management, and succession management strategies. Teaching leaders both coaching and mentorship is essential, and organizations must strike a balance between these programs when developing their leadership initiatives.

Case Study

Ali had been a senior manager for eight years. She knew the business and operations inside out. She was well-versed in handling problems and loved helping her team solve them. Problem-solving was her strength, and supporting her team on the job brought her a sense of fulfillment.

However, feedback from her team indicated that she was micromanaging, which left her frustrated. In response, she pulled back, only to receive new feedback that she wasn't coaching her team enough.

This back-and-forth left both Ali and her team frustrated. They felt stuck between her micromanaging and a distant, too delegative approach. Recognizing the need for change, Ali decided to seek coaching for herself.

Her company hired a coach, and together they identified key focus areas for Ali's development. Based on these areas, Ali was also encouraged to take a comprehensive coaching course.

Through her training and coaching sessions, Ali learned how to apply situational leadership. She developed the ability to balance coaching and mentoring, using both approaches depending on the situation and the individual.

She realized that some issues and certain team members required hands-on leadership, where working together directly to solve problems was appreciated and most effective. In other cases, she needed to ask questions, guide the employee to find their own solutions, and explore their needs, showing support and trust in the process.

What You Can Do

- Understand what coaching is: Embrace coaching as a learning and development strategy and move beyond its tactical usage. Clarify your coaching strategy, make coaching programs a regular budget item, and prioritize their importance.
- Implement coaching into your programs: Expand your learning programs to have coaching components focusing on implementing learnings.
- Get coached: Experience being coached, which will complement the process of becoming a coach leader.
- Build a coaching culture: If you are in a senior leadership position, work with HR to develop a coaching strategy, clarify your approach to bringing in external coaches and build the internal coaching capacity of your leaders and managers.

Growth Need: Belief in Potential

Statement: My leader believes in me.

This need/statement assesses whether employees feel their leader believes in their potential and supports their professional development. This may include demonstrating confidence in their abilities, encouraging them to take on new challenges, and recognizing their achievements.

In our initial qualitative research, we asked participants to reflect on moments when they felt they were "at their best" and "fully utilizing their potential." In some cases, we directly inquired about times they felt "self-actualized."

Although their examples varied, one theme was consistent: a leader played a key role in enabling these experiences. Participants described such leaders as "empowering," "trusting," and someone who "believed in them."

When we asked participants to elaborate on what these leaders were doing, they described their leaders as great coaches and/or mentors. These leaders believed in human potential and actively helped them reach their best selves. Their role went beyond simple delegation—they worked alongside their people, helping them identify their North Star and guiding them toward it. In short, the leader as a coach is a crucial role in enabling individuals and teams to move towards self-actualization.

Real-Life Example

At a consulting company I worked for, I had two leaders who recognized my creativity and ability to challenge the status quo. I was keen to develop my own way of doing things, and since I wasn't in a junior role, they trusted me to develop my own approach. They gave me the flexibility to shape my work, especially in client acquisition and other tasks, and I was delivering results. I can confidently say my approach was working.

However, when the leadership changed, so did the environment. My new leader formed an impression of me before we ever met, gathering feedback from others in the office rather than getting to know me personally. That was her way of gathering intelligence about those in the office; by hearing what others had to say.

In our first 1:1 meeting, she had already formed an impression about me. In some cases, learning other colleagues' perspectives may be valuable to build a strong leadership approach. Yet, in our first conversation, she used the information to dismiss my strengths entirely. She acknowledged hearing about my creativity but then told me she needed "cookie cutters" on her team. She wanted things done her way and asked if I could commit to that.

She never took the time to get to know me or build proper trust. She asked me to be a cookie cutter, knowing that I was a creative person. To this day, this is one of my corporate traumas. I still get goosebumps thinking about it.

For me, it led to high levels of workplace anxiety and burnout. Eventually, I decided to leave the organization, as the team's culture shifted from friendly and collaborative one to a cut-throat, "get results at all costs" culture. It made me realize how much leaders can make a difference in the employee experience—they truly make it or break it. I am so glad I left that organization.

Senior leaders may think that because they have a larger culture strategy, all the leaders are applying it in the same way. That's simply not true, and I have experienced it.

The leader you're working for makes such a difference, and our research reflects that. There was no concern for me or my needs, and it was dehumanizing. I felt like a cog in the machine. I tried to hold on to the hope that I could still add value by fitting the cookie-cutter mold, but deep down, I knew it wasn't right for me, and I couldn't force it. I left the company six months later.

People are becoming more aware of this, and The Great Resignation shows that they're seeking organizations that treat them with humanity. They want to work for workplaces that cover their basic needs and build non-toxic cultures. They want to work for leaders who help them flourish and thrive. Many organizations lack this approach, leading to retention struggles they can't fully understand.

I often hear it reduced to the fact that "everyone is so unappreciative," but it's the responsibility of leaders and organizations to adapt to the changing paradigm and equip themselves with the right tools.

It's like working with old software and wondering why your computer is slow. Humanity has progressed— needs have progressed. All leaders and organizations must understand this, or they will fail.

We have seen many large corporations fail in wake of the pandemic because of their stubbornness to change. I left that company because my leader didn't prioritize my needs, and the culture had changed. It wasn't the same organization I had joined years earlier. Don't get me wrong, change can be good. However, this leader didn't just alter my experience, she negatively impacted the entire team and the workplace culture. I wasn't the only one who chose to resign.

What You Can Do

- Genuinely get to know your employees: The first step in proving that you believe in someone's potential is to understand their goals and passions. If you know what they want to achieve, you can help them get there.

- Identify their strengths and weaknesses: Encourage them to take on roles that may challenge them and be opportunities for growth.
- Demonstrate confidence in their abilities: Don't shy away from giving employees difficult tasks and support them when they feel self-doubt.
- Reward and congratulate them for accomplishments: It is brave to take on new tasks and to challenge yourself. Make sure your employees know that you appreciate them going the extra mile.

In this chapter, I reviewed the research findings on growth needs at work. Growth needs ended up being primarily based on our relationship with our direct supervisor. I am considering re-naming the growth needs as leadership needs, as all the statements/needs focus on leadership behaviors.

In my opinion, the most significant finding from this research is that people care less about the organization's purpose or its "why" and more about whether their leader is purposeful and consistently models their purpose and the organization's values. This shift in focus is a significant departure from the current rhetoric, which emphasizes spending excessive time and energy on crafting an organizational purpose.

A leader might know about the concepts of authentic leadership, servant leadership, emotional intelligence, and empathy. Yet, knowing is not enough. People want to work for leaders that role model and embody those concepts.

From North Star to Lived Experience: Aligning Culture Across All Levels of Leadership

As we close this part on understanding basic needs, psychological needs and growth needs in the workplace, I want to revisit the purpose of this research: to expand our understanding of what workplace culture is. The current approach used in many organizations today is what I call "culture as a north star." This understanding of culture builds on values and vision and how leaders role model them. While this is a fundamental facet of culture, it is not the only one. The biggest disconnect lies in the fact that employees view culture as their lived experience, while many leaders see it as the north star.

Understanding employee experience is no easy task. I often hear leaders, managers, and supervisors express confusion, saying, 'I don't understand these people,' far more than they express understanding them. This doesn't mean we have to agree all the time, but understanding is a sign of empathy, whereas a lack of understanding indicates disconnect. To build cohesive, high-performing, people-focused teams, we need leaders who understand the collective needs of their team members. Leading with culture addresses this challenge.

In 2023 and 2024, we had the opportunity to prototype and further implement the leading with culture methodology in highly reputable organizations in North

America. The feedback consistently signaled that we're on the right track.

In one project, one of the sponsor executives commented that everything we shared aligned with his observations. Beyond that, he mentioned how we helped him find voice and language to explain what he had been noticing. This whole organization was trained on leading with culture, using data-driven insights specific to their environment. Culture action plans were developed for the top three levels of the organization, and key leaders received coaching that held them accountable for role modeling the desired behaviors.

One year later, we were contacted by a sister organization connected to the team we had been working with. While the leaders of both organizations had communicated about the success of our program, what truly made an impact was the firsthand feedback from a mid-level leader who had gone through the program. The executive leader of the new organization had been mentoring this mid-level leader for a decade. Over the past year, she had witnessed significant growth in his leadership capabilities, which he attributed directly to the coaching and cultural work we had done. This personal transformation, more than top-down praise, was the game changer that convinced them to reach out. They were eager to learn more about our work, having seen the significant transformation it had created, and were interested in implementing a similar program within their organization. We are thrilled to see another organization embracing the 'leading with culture' approach among their changemakers.

CHAPTER 6

The Operational Culture Index©

Having grasped and built a tool that measures culture from an employee needs perspective, it was time to take the next step: exploring how organizational operations shape workplace culture. The Operational Culture Index© was the next tool to be developed in our holistic approach to understand and measure culture.

Origins

My understanding of culture as operational fabric developed over many years facilitating workshops on efficiency. An Ishikawa diagram, often called a fishbone diagram, is typically used to conduct root cause analysis by asking a series of "why" questions. In various industries with different contexts and cultures, I noticed that in these operational efficiency discussions, there was always at least one element of team communication and several others on the team's experience. Although the focus was on product quality or the efficiency and value-add of a process, aspects of the employee experience consistently affected operations.

Over time, I started noticing the impact operations had on the employees' experience, leading me to coin the term operational culture. Since 2020, I have been conducting workshops on this topic under the name Operational Culture Levers©. These levers include strategy (how strategy is operationalized), structure (how the organization is structured), decision-making (how the decision-making and power dynamics work), leaders (whether leaders have the right knowledge, skills, and abilities), people (whether employees have the right knowledge, skills, and abilities), processes (clear operational processes and well defined operational procedures), policies & practices (an understanding of the human resources element), and systems (whether employees have the right tools and technologies to do their jobs). A few colleagues who attended these workshops highlighted the similarities with McKinsey's 7S framework. It's a good sign to see convergence on similar topics when replicated in different times and geographies.

Several participants shared that they found the topics and the probing question very impactful and a great foundation for building high-performing operations with a people-focused perspective.

The Operational Culture Levers© later evolved as an input to the Operational Culture Index© research. My findings on the eight facets of operational culture informed our research team on the clusters, which then, through subject matter expert consultation, turned into statements for each of the eight topics. While two of these levers emerged as the main drivers of operational culture, we still facilitate the workshop on all eight. After these sessions, we review the results for the two key drivers and analyze how employees responded to those two pillars to further understand their significance.

To connect the dots, operational culture is an aspect of the broader organizational culture, shaped by the daily experiences of how the work is carried out within the company. It's reflected in the way tasks are executed—from handling logistics to answering calls. It encompasses how strategy is communicated, how decisions are made, who rises to leadership, and how policies and procedures are developed. It shapes how an organization functions at its core.

Keeping the employee experience in mind, we began further research to understand the Operational Culture Index$^©$. This tool was developed to complement the Culture-Actualization Index$^©$ in our approach and evaluation of an organization's workplace culture. Only by capturing both aspects can organizations truly understand the influence of culture in their organization and harness it to drive performance and unity.

The Research

In this section, I will give a brief overview of our extensive research into operational culture and the development of the Operational Culture Index$^©$. For a detailed description of our research process for the OCI, please see Appendix B.

Much like the CAI, the preliminary qualitative research started the OCI index development. After clearly understanding the eight pillars and their crucial role in developing operational workplace culture, I defined forty-three survey statements within these categories.

All categories affect each other in some way; for example, you must have effective leadership and strategy to carry out efficient systems and processes. Understanding how these factors affect each other and the employees of an organization is crucial to building and maintaining a healthy workplace culture.

After the successful completion of the CAI in partnership with Saint Mary's University and Mitacs, we partnered with these organizations once again and began the next step in the research process.

The survey statements derived from the qualitative research were then put to the test; we conducted a study involving subject matter experts to validate these items. This process allowed us to eliminate inaccurate statements and reduce our list to forty-three items. Most importantly, this first phase of our research validated that the Operational Culture Index© accurately measured the intended eight factors and therefore, could evaluate workplace culture.

Phase two of our research consisted of a two-wave study that further analyzed and validated our survey in various ways. We found that of the eight categories, two were significant; structure and systems. The statements within these categories were reduced to seven, further refining and concentrating the tool as a whole.

Findings

Following the research and development phases of the Operational Culture Index© (OCI), further studies highlighted the increasing significance of two critical categories: systems and structure. These pillars emerged as statistically significant drivers in fostering a high-performing operational culture. In this chapter, we will delve into these findings and introduce the seven new statements that were crafted to measure these aspects of organizational culture.

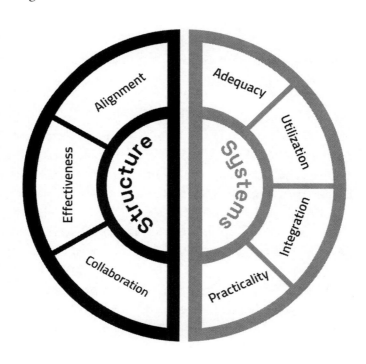

Structure: A well-designed framework for success

The first category that surfaced as a key driver was structure. A well-defined organizational structure fosters collaboration, clear decision-making processes, and alignment across teams. In fact, structure plays a crucial role in reducing ambiguity in roles and responsibilities, which directly impacts both team cohesion and operational outcomes.

Structure: Collaboration

Statement: Different parts of the organization's structure work well together to achieve common goals.

This statement assesses whether employees feel that the organization's structure facilitates effective collaboration across teams and departments. When the structure is clear, aligned, and designed to promote communication and cooperation, employees are better able to work together toward shared goals. On the other hand, a disjointed or siloed structure can hinder teamwork, slow decision-making, and create barriers to achieving organizational objectives.

Organizations with an effective structure foster seamless collaboration between departments, ensuring that everyone understands their roles and how their work contributes to the larger mission. A clear structure creates accountability while empowering employees to collaborate without unnecessary layers of complexity.

Case Study

Samantha works in the marketing department of a large retail company. Although her department is highly skilled, they often struggle to coordinate with the product development and sales teams. The organizational structure separates these teams into different silos, making cross-department collaboration difficult. Requests for input on new campaigns are delayed as emails bounce between various managers, and decisions that require input from multiple teams often take weeks.

Frustrated by the lack of cohesion, Samantha suggests creating a cross-department project group that meets regularly to align on marketing, product development, and sales strategies. However, the company's rigid structure makes it difficult to implement her suggestion, as each department has different reporting lines and approval processes.

Without a structure that promotes collaboration, Samantha and her colleagues continue to face bottlenecks, and the company misses opportunities to bring innovative products to market quickly. After a particularly frustrating experience where a key campaign was delayed by poor cross-department communication, Samantha begins considering whether a more collaborative environment elsewhere would be a better fit for her skills.

What You Can Do

- Foster cross-department teams: Create opportunities for departments to work together on projects or initiatives. Establish regular meetings or task forces where representatives from different areas of the organization can align on goals and share information.

- Clarify roles and reporting lines: Ensure that employees across departments understand how their roles interact and where to go for input or approvals. Simplifying reporting structures can reduce delays and improve accountability.
- Break down silos: Encourage collaboration by rewarding teamwork and breaking down any barriers that prevent teams from working together. This might include adjusting the organizational chart to ensure that departments with overlapping responsibilities are aligned more closely.
- Facilitate communication: Use collaborative tools and platforms to streamline communication between departments. Make sure that employees have easy access to the information and contacts they need to collaborate effectively.

Structure: Effectiveness

Statement: The decision-making process within the structure is effective.

This statement measures whether employees feel that decisions are made quickly, efficiently, and in a transparent manner. Efficient decision-making ensures that teams can move forward with projects without unnecessary delays, while transparency helps build trust between employees and leadership.

A lack of clarity or excessive bureaucracy in decision-making can lead to delays, frustration, and reduced employee engagement.

Case Study

Sarah, a product manager at a retail company, often finds herself waiting weeks for decisions to be made on important product updates. The company's decision-making process is bogged down by multiple layers of approval, with little communication on how or when final decisions will be made.

The constant delays not only slow down product launches but also frustrate Sarah's team, which struggles to stay motivated while waiting for feedback. The lack of transparency around decision-making leaves the team feeling out of the loop and disconnected from company leadership.

Eventually, Sarah grows tired of the inefficiency and begins looking for a company with a more agile and transparent approach to decision-making.

What You Can Do

- Streamline the decision-making process: Simplify approval processes to reduce unnecessary delays and empower teams to make decisions more quickly.
- Increase transparency: Clearly communicate who is responsible for making decisions and the timeline for when decisions will be made, ensuring that employees feel informed.

- Empower teams: Delegate decision-making authority to teams or departments where appropriate, allowing them to make faster, more informed decisions.

Structure: Alignment

Statement: The executive team is aligned on governance principles.

This statement assesses whether employees feel that the executive leadership team operates with a shared understanding of governance principles and organizational direction. When the executive team is aligned, it fosters consistency in decision-making, policies, and communication, which helps create stability and confidence across the organization.

Misalignment among executives can lead to mixed messages, unclear priorities, and reduced trust within the workforce.

Case Study

David works in human resources for a large financial services firm. Recently, he's noticed that the executive team seems divided on key issues, with conflicting messages being sent to employees about strategic priorities. One day, the CEO announces a new initiative focused on innovation, while the CFO stresses cost-cutting measures that contradict this vision.

The lack of alignment at the executive level creates confusion and frustration for David and his colleagues, as they are unsure which direction to follow. Morale begins to drop as employees question the company's leadership and its future direction.

David brings up his concerns in an HR meeting, but there is little acknowledgment of the misalignment at the top. Frustrated by the lack of coherent leadership, David starts considering whether a company with stronger executive alignment would be a better fit for his career.

What You Can Do

- Foster open communication among executives: Ensure that the executive team regularly meets to align on key governance principles and organizational goals, and that any disagreements are resolved before communicating with the broader organization.
- Create a unified leadership message: Develop consistent messaging from the top down, so that employees receive clear, coherent direction from leadership.
- Model alignment for the rest of the organization: When the executive team is aligned, it sets a positive example for the rest of the company, promoting consistency and cohesion at all levels.

Systems: The Backbone of Operational Excellence

One of our research's most notable outcomes was identifying systems as a fundamental driver of operational culture. As organizations grow and diversify, the systems they utilize—whether technological or procedural—become the framework upon which day-to-day operations rely. Our research confirmed that systems not only influence operational efficiency but also play a pivotal role in shaping employee satisfaction and engagement.

Systems: Practicality

Statement: Procedures are practical.

This factor assesses whether procedures within the organization are practical. It measures the efficiency and effectiveness of organizational processes and how well they support the daily tasks of employees. It may include regularly reviewing and updating procedures to eliminate redundancies, simplifying workflows, and ensuring that processes are user-friendly and align with the organization's objectives.

In organizations with well-designed procedures, employees report feeling more empowered and less stressed, as the processes they follow are clear and logical. On the other hand, poorly defined or overly complex procedures can create frustration and reduce productivity, leading to disengagement and job dissatisfaction.

Case Study

Rachel works as a project manager at a midsized technology firm. Over the past year, her team has struggled to keep up with client expectations, not due to lack of effort, but because the internal procedures for delivering projects are overly complicated. Every time a new client project begins, Rachel spends days navigating approval processes and ensuring all necessary documents are filled out—a task that could take hours with a more streamlined approach.

Although Rachel brings up the issue during team meetings, her suggestions for simplifying procedures are often ignored. This leaves her frustrated, as she knows that time spent managing unnecessary paperwork could be better used improving client relations and ensuring quality project outcomes.

Rachel's stress increases as she watches her team struggle with similar challenges. Eventually, a senior colleague leaves the company, citing frustration with the time-wasting procedures as one of the main reasons. With no change in sight, Rachel begins exploring other job opportunities where more practical systems and procedures are in place, hoping to find a workplace that allows her to focus on what she does best—leading projects.

What You Can Do

- Streamline procedures: Review your current processes to ensure they are as simple and practical as possible. Employees should not spend excessive time navigating complex systems just to complete basic tasks. Aim to reduce redundancy and simplify workflows wherever possible.

- Encourage employee feedback: Create a system where employees can provide feedback on existing procedures, and regularly review and update processes based on their input. This ensures that the people closest to the work are helping shape the systems they use.
- Test and adjust: Before implementing a new procedure, test it on a small scale. Gather insights from users to identify any potential issues, then adjust the procedure accordingly before rolling it out organization wide.
- Train for efficiency: Once practical procedures are in place, ensure that employees are well-trained on how to use them efficiently. A process is only as effective as the team's ability to navigate it smoothly.

Systems: Integration

Statement: Systems are well-integrated with each other.

This factor measures how well systems are integrated with each other. It evaluates the seamlessness of communication and data flow between different software, hardware, and technological platforms within the organization. It may include selecting compatible technologies, implementing standardized protocols, and ensuring regular maintenance and updates.

Disjointed systems, on the other hand, can lead to delays, errors, and frustration, ultimately lowering employee productivity and engagement.

Case Study

Ahmed works in customer support at a global logistics company. His team relies on several different software platforms to manage customer inquiries, shipments, and payment processing. Unfortunately, these systems aren't integrated, which means Ahmed often has to manually transfer information from one system to another, leading to delays and mistakes.

One day, an important client's shipment is delayed because the payment processing system didn't communicate with the inventory system. Ahmed spends hours troubleshooting the issue, feeling increasingly frustrated with how these disjointed systems are negatively impacting both his work and customer satisfaction.

When Ahmed voices his concerns to his manager, he's told that system integration is expensive, but no steps are taken to address the issue. The inefficiencies continue to affect Ahmed's daily work, contributing to his growing dissatisfaction with the company.

What You Can Do

- Invest in integration tools: Implement platforms or middleware that connect different systems, ensuring smooth data flow between departments and reducing the need for manual intervention.

- Regularly review system effectiveness: Conduct periodic reviews to assess whether current systems are effectively meeting the organization's needs and where integration might improve performance.
- Provide training on system usage: Ensure employees are well-trained on how to use integrated systems and how to troubleshoot common issues, so they can operate efficiently without relying on workarounds.

Systems: Utilization

Statement: Systems are being well-used by employees.

This statement assesses whether employees are using the systems available to them efficiently and correctly. Well-utilized systems enhance productivity and streamline workflows, while underused or misused systems can create bottlenecks, reduce efficiency, and increase frustration.

Ensuring that employees are properly trained on how to use systems and that those systems meet their day-to-day needs is critical to operational success.

Case Study

Emma, a sales executive at a tech firm, is frustrated with the company's customer relationship management (CRM) system. Although the CRM is designed to track client interactions and sales progress, many of her colleagues find it confusing and avoid using it. As a result, key updates are missed, and information becomes scattered across different platforms, creating inefficiencies.

Emma sees the potential of the CRM to streamline workflows and enhance team collaboration. She raises the issue with her manager, suggesting a comprehensive training program to help employees better understand and use the system. She also proposes appointing "CRM champions" within each team to support ongoing system usage and share best practices.

After some initial hesitation, leadership agrees to invest in Emma's suggestion, recognizing the long-term benefits of proper system utilization. The company rolls out a series of training sessions, led by internal CRM champions, to ensure that everyone is comfortable with the system. They also introduce periodic reviews to monitor usage and offer additional support as needed.

Within a few months, the entire sales team is using the CRM effectively, and communication has vastly improved. Information is now centralized, making it easier for everyone to track client interactions and follow up on leads. The streamlined workflow leads to faster decision-making and better client outcomes, and Emma's productivity increases as a result.

Pleased with the changes, Emma feels more engaged in her role and confident in the company's direction. The organization benefits from smoother processes and increased sales performance, demonstrating the value of investing in employee training and system utilization.

What You Can Do

- Provide comprehensive system training: Ensure all employees are trained on how to use systems effectively and offer ongoing support for troubleshooting and best practices.
- Monitor system usage: Use analytics to track how well systems are being used and identify any gaps in usage or adoption across the organization.
- Make systems user-friendly: Regularly assess whether the systems in place are meeting employee needs and, if necessary, modify or replace them with more intuitive options.

Systems: Adequacy

Statement: The systems in place meet organizational needs.

This statement evaluates whether employees feel that the organization's systems are well-suited to the demands of their jobs and the overall business. When systems are aligned with organizational needs, they help employees perform their tasks efficiently, contributing to overall productivity and success. When systems are outdated or do not support the company's evolving goals, they can become barriers to operational efficiency.

Case Study

Juan, an operations manager at a manufacturing company, oversees the coordination of shipments and inventory management. Recently, the company implemented a new inventory management system, but it wasn't designed to handle the complexity of their global supply chain. As a result, tracking inventory and coordinating shipments across regions has become increasingly difficult, leading to production delays.

Juan spends hours each week creating workarounds to manage the system's limitations, which pulls him away from more strategic tasks. Despite his best efforts, operational issues persist, causing missed deadlines and frustrated clients.

Frustrated with the system's inefficiencies, Juan raises his concerns with senior management. Initially, the response is hesitant due to the costs involved in replacing the system. However, after Juan presents a detailed report highlighting the lost productivity, missed opportunities, and client dissatisfaction caused by the system's inadequacies, management agrees to reconsider.

The company decides to bring in a team of consultants to assess their current operations and recommend upgrades or adjustments. After a thorough evaluation, the company opts to integrate additional features into their existing system rather than replacing it entirely. The enhanced system is tailored to meet the specific needs of their global supply chain, ensuring that tracking and coordination run smoothly.

Within months, production delays are significantly reduced, and Juan can refocus on more strategic, value-added tasks. The improvements not only boost operational efficiency but also improve client satisfaction. Juan feels a renewed sense of confidence in the company's commitment to growth and its ability to adapt to evolving business needs.

What You Can Do

- Assess system suitability regularly: Evaluate whether the systems in place still meet the evolving needs of the organization, especially as the company grows or changes direction.
- Solicit employee feedback: Gather input from employees to understand how well systems support their day-to-day tasks and where improvements are needed.
- Adapt systems to business changes: As the organization grows or shifts focus, ensure that systems are updated or replaced to meet new operational requirements.

People: The Heart of Operational Culture

Our research revealed a third category: the People. The factor emerged as statistically significant, highlighting its crucial role in shaping operational culture. While this category clearly impacts employee engagement, retention, and satisfaction, we are still working to fully understand its nuances, especially in relation to the Culture-Actualization Index© (CAI), which is centered on the human experience and leadership behavior that affect employees directly. Given the complexity of how organizational culture affects individuals, more research is needed to explore how the People factor in the OCI complements or diverges from the CAI, allowing us to deepen our understanding in future iterations of our analysis.

Human Needs and Operational Culture: The Relationship Between OCI and CAI

In the final phase of our work, we explored how the Operational Culture Index© (OCI) and the Culture-Actualization Index© (CAI) interact to offer a fuller picture of organizational culture. This phase involved various analyses to understand the relationship between the two tools—how closely they align, their distinct factor structures, and their ability to predict outcomes over time.

Earlier, in phase two, our study revealed that higher OCI scores correlated strongly with increased creativity, job satisfaction, work engagement, and loyalty. There was a moderate link between the OCI and factors like trust and organizational commitment, while job performance showed only a weak connection, suggesting OCI is not a direct indicator of this metric. Perhaps most importantly, we found that the OCI had a moderate negative relationship with turnover, meaning higher OCI scores are associated with lower turnover rates. A high OCI score therefore corresponds to lower turnover rates, just like the CAI.

In this final phase, we confirmed that the OCI and CAI are not only strongly aligned but also measure distinct elements of culture. A high score in one typically indicates a high score in the other, yet each captures unique aspects of the organizational experience. There was another key finding that reinforced this idea; the research found that the OCI highlights current cultural strengths and weaknesses, while the CAI monitors the long-term impact and sustainability of cultural initiatives.

Together, these tools offer a comprehensive view of workplace culture, and each tool enhances the value of the other. By using them in tandem, leaders can gain deeper insights into both the immediate and lasting effects of cultural practices within their organizations. Ultimately, the OCI complements the CAI, helping leaders build workplaces grounded in strong cultural foundations.

CHAPTER 7

Leading with Culture: Practices, Listening, and Change

The Power of Cultural Practices

As companies strive for excellence, the importance of cultural practices becomes crucial in shaping environments where both people and businesses thrive. But what exactly are cultural practices, and why are they so critical to a thriving workplace culture?

Cultural practices go beyond surface-level interactions; they are tangible expressions of a group's collective values. They manifest through three key elements: symbols, rituals, and heroes. These elements bring life to an organization's values and identity. They provide a framework for how employees interact, make decisions, and approach their work daily. Understanding these practices and their role in workplace culture is fundamental to any leader aiming to create lasting cultural impact.

Symbols

Logos, names, and visuals that represent the essence of your organization's identity. These elements may seem unrelated at first glance, but they often carry deep meaning and act as powerful reminders of the company's mission and values.

Heroes

Every organization has its heroes—they are the success stories, best practices, learnings, and insights that inspire and guide your team. These embody the culture you aim to cultivate. Heroes are examples of cultural values in action, and they inspire others to set ambitious goals.

Rituals

Rituals are the repeated, shared behaviors that reinforce the organization's values. From meetings to company-wide celebrations, these rituals serve as cultural anchors that create consistency, meaning, and culture on a daily basis.

Understanding Values through Cultural Practices

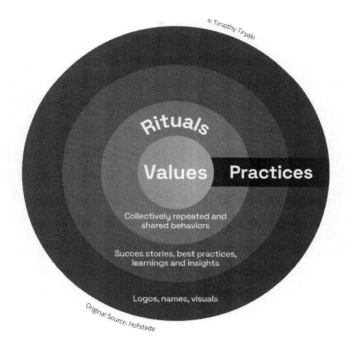

As leaders, it's not enough to merely understand these elements. The task at hand is to assess the current cultural practices in place and intentionally shape them to align with your organization's evolving goals and values.

Begin by observing the symbols, heroes, and rituals that already exist within your organization. What stories do they tell about your culture? Do they align with your desired values, or do they reinforce an outdated narrative? For example, the company logo may have a long history, but does it still resonate with your current identity? Likewise, consider the unsung heroes, the success stories, within your company—are their contributions aligned with where you want to take your team?

Next, you must evaluate whether the existing practices are supporting or undermining your cultural objectives. Just because a symbol or ritual has been around for a while doesn't mean it's still effective. Sometimes, practices that were once vital to the organization can become counterproductive if left unchecked. Leaders need to adapt, phase out, or reframe these practices to ensure they serve the company's current and future needs.

Innovation is key when building a culture that reflects your organization's aspirations. This involves introducing new symbols, recognizing fresh heroes, and creating rituals that resonate with both the leadership and the workforce. Whether it's establishing new awards, formalizing new team daily tasks, or amplifying voices that embody the company's ethos, these practices must be meaningful and relevant to the workforce.

Successfully identifying, evaluating, and building cultural practices requires more than just intention. It requires a systemic approach. Your culture should not exist in isolation; it should actively support and accelerate the strategic objectives and values of the organization. While leaders may guide cultural practices and role model them, employees are the ones who breathe life into the daily culture. Engage your teams in the process of creating new symbols, rituals, and identifying the heroes within the organization. This collective approach fosters a stronger sense of ownership and commitment.

Like any business function, culture must be measured to be improved. The Maslow Culture Index was developed from this need; to help leaders assess the efficacy of cultural practices, from operational aspects to the needs of employees within the organization. Measuring these factors ensures that leaders can make data-informed decisions about how to refine and evolve the culture over time.

Great cultures aren't built by accident. They are the result of deliberate choices made by leaders who understand the profound role that cultural practices play in shaping the organization's future.

Listening Strategies

In addition to cultural practices, a successful leader must also cultivate an organizational listening strategy that captures the voices of employees. This strategy ensures that the cultural shifts you aim to foster are aligned with the evolving needs of your workforce.

It's clear that employees increasingly want to work for organizations and leaders that value their input and tap into the collective intelligence of the workforce. However, this doesn't mean that every decision needs to be made by consensus. Rather, the most respected leadership style is one that listens to diverse perspectives, makes informed decisions, and clearly communicates the reasoning behind those decisions.

The foundation for this type of leadership begins with a strong organizational listening strategy. Such a strategy is critical for cultivating a culture where employees feel valued and heard, ultimately fostering higher engagement, retention, and innovation.

Listening, in the context of leadership, is more than just a passive act. It requires creating systems and processes that actively seek out employee voices, not just during moments of crisis or transition, but as an ongoing practice. Leaders who excel in this area are not merely conduits for feedback but architects of a culture that encourages and rewards openness and transparency.

The key is finding the balance between listening and decision-making. Employees appreciate leaders who not only seek their opinions but also explain how those perspectives shape final decisions. This clarity and accountability create a stronger connection between leadership and the workforce, driving a culture of trust and mutual respect.

To build an effective and wholesome organizational listening strategy, leaders need to implement structured methods for gathering insights and feedback from employees across all levels. A multi-faceted approach ensures that different voices are heard, and that leaders can act on feedback in meaningful ways. Below are some of the most effective strategies.

Organizational Listening Strategies

© Timothy Tiryaki

Annual Surveys & Pulse Surveys
Overall organizational health, culture and climate checkups

Inclusive Meeting Culture
Check-in meetings, consultation meetings, and closing meetings

Exit Interviews
Feedback on reasons for leaving/quitting the company

Manager Once Removed Connections
With employees at least 2 levels down

Town Halls
Q&A segments with leaders and/or managers

Listening Labs/ Listening Circles
Creating listening circles opportunities for specific needs

Field Visits
Employee/worker site visits, or Client/Customer/Consumer visits

Sentiment Analysis from Communcation
Using written emails and chat analysis

Annual Surveys & Pulse Surveys

Regular surveys provide an overall health check of the organization's culture and climate. Annual surveys offer comprehensive feedback, while pulse surveys, conducted more frequently, provide real-time insights into employee morale and engagement. These tools allow leaders to track trends and respond proactively to any emerging issues.

Exit Interviews

Exit interviews are an often underutilized but critical source of insight. Understanding the reasons why employees choose to leave an organization can reveal underlying cultural issues that may not surface through regular surveys. By capturing this information, leaders can address systemic problems before they affect retention on a larger scale.

Town Halls

Open forums, such as town halls, provide a platform for employees to ask questions and express concerns directly to leadership. These Q&A sessions promote transparency, foster two-way communication, and build trust, as employees see leaders addressing their questions in real time.

Field Visits

In-person engagement, through site visits or client/ customer visits, helps leaders get a firsthand view of workplace dynamics. By seeing employees in action, leaders gain a deeper understanding of the challenges they face and can better align strategic decisions with the on-the-ground reality.

Inclusive Meeting Culture

Meetings should not just be platforms for top-down communication. By incorporating elements like check-in circles, consultation circles, and closing circles, leaders can ensure that employees' voices are heard throughout the decision-making process. These inclusive practices make meetings more collaborative and less hierarchical.

Manager Once Removed Connections

This practice involves leaders connecting with employees at least two levels down in the organization. These conversations offer insights into how policies and decisions made at higher levels are affecting those further down the chain of command. They also provide a platform for employees to feel recognized and heard by senior leadership.

Listening Labs / Listening Circles

These are specific consultation opportunities where leaders can explore particular issues or topics with employees. By setting up topic-specific labs or circles, organizations can gather focused feedback that may not surface through more general surveys or town halls.

Sentiment Analysis from Written Communication

Sentiment analysis allows organizations to mine written communication (emails, chats) for patterns in employee attitudes and emotions. This method provides an additional layer of insight into workplace culture, particularly when employees may not feel comfortable expressing their thoughts in more formal settings.

Building a robust listening strategy is not just about collecting data—it's about integrating listening into the fabric of the organization. By actively listening, leaders show employees that their perspectives matter and that their input helps shape the organization's future. This approach fosters a people-centered culture where employees feel invested, respected, and motivated to contribute their best work.

At its core, a strong organizational listening strategy helps leaders build not only a great workplace culture but also a resilient and adaptive organization. By listening to employees, leaders gain insights that can drive innovation, improve engagement, and create a sense of shared purpose within the organization.

In the end, organizations that listen—truly listen—are the ones that thrive.

The Being Plan and The Doing Plan

Action planning is one of the critical steps in strategy execution, ensuring that organizational objectives are translated into actionable steps. However, one often overlooked facet of this process is the role of leadership role modeling in achieving success. While action plans traditionally focus on tasks, timelines, and responsibilities, there's a deeper, more profound component that connects leadership behaviors and values with strategic outcomes.

At the heart of every action plan lies a structured approach—objectives, initiatives, and projects, typically detailed with a RASCI framework (Responsible, Accountable, Supporting, Consulted, Informed) and SMARTER goals (Specific, Measurable, Achievable, Relevant, Time-bound, Evaluated, Reviewed). This forms the doing side of action planning, where the emphasis is on execution and measurable progress.

However, this "doing" side tells only half of the story. For over 15 years, I have pioneered the integration of what

I call the "being plan," a concept designed to elevate action planning by embedding leadership values, behaviors, and cultural practices into the strategic framework.

Leadership is not solely about achieving results—it's about identity, purpose, and influence. The being plan forms the foundation of this identity by aligning who leaders are with what they do. This plan emphasizes three key areas: values, leadership behaviors, and cultural practices. Values represent the core beliefs that guide decision-making and define the organization's ethos. Leadership behaviors are the observable actions that reflect these values and influence others. Cultural practices, such as shared rituals, symbols, and stories, reinforce the organization's culture and shape interactions between leaders and employees.

Strategic Objectives

The purpose of an action plan lies at the core of the model—realizing the strategic objectives. These objectives are the guideposts that align day-to-day activities with the company's mission, vision, and long-term goals. In our approach to strategy, based on Dr. Jeroen Kraaijenbrink's work, we use a model called the Joint Strategic View (JSV) to help organizations crystallize their vision and align it with their strategic objectives. Through the Strategy Sketch˙ framework, we design this view, ensuring that it is both actionable and aligned with the organization's mission. Additionally, we connect the JSV with the organization's North Star through the North Star Canvas˙, ensuring that every objective supports the broader organizational purpose.

These strategic objectives serve as the foundation for both the Doing and Being Plans, creating a roadmap that leaders and employees can follow with clarity and focus.

To fully realize an organization's strategic objectives, both the Doing and Being Plans must work in tandem. Each serves a distinct yet complementary purpose:

The Doing Plan

This is the traditional part of action planning that centers on tangible execution. It outlines specific initiatives, actions, and KPIs that are necessary to achieve the strategic goals. The Doing Plan provides the framework for measurable progress and defines the steps needed to execute the strategy effectively.

The Being Plan

This aspect of planning transcends the tactical to focus on leadership identity. It emphasizes values, behaviors, and cultural practices that shape leadership and drive a high-performance mindset. The Being Plan fosters an environment where leadership is rooted in authenticity, with leaders who embody the organization's values and influence others through their actions.

By focusing on both "doing" and "being," leaders create not only the conditions for success but also the mindset and cultural alignment necessary to sustain it. This dual approach recognizes that strategy isn't just a matter of tasks and KPIs—it's about aligning leadership behavior with the organization's values to create lasting impact.

The being plan is not a substitute for the action-oriented doing plan; rather, it complements it by ensuring that leadership behaviors align with organizational values, which in turn supports the achievement of strategic goals. Together, the being plan and doing plan create a holistic approach to leadership and strategy execution.

The true power of this approach lies in its integration. A well-executed strategy must reflect both who leaders are and what they aim to accomplish. The Doing Plan and the Being Plan are two sides of the same coin—one focusing on the concrete actions needed to achieve goals, and the other grounding those actions in a foundation of strong leadership and cultural alignment.

This integrated model recognizes that leadership is both a set of behaviors and a reflection of values. It is this combination that creates a sustainable path to achieving strategic objectives.

Action planning is about more than just ticking off tasks—it's about aligning leadership behavior with the organization's broader mission and values. By adopting this dual approach, leaders can ensure that they are not only executing strategies effectively but also fostering a culture of leadership that inspires and sustains high performance.

The integration of the Being Plan with the Doing Plan brings together the best of both worlds, enabling organizations to achieve their strategic objectives while building a leadership culture that is authentic, value-driven, and sustainable.

At the end of the day, strategy is not accidental. It's who we are and what we do.

Transformation and Stability Management: Beyond Typical Change Management

I started this book by acknowledging that change is constant and inevitable. But again, successful strategy execution is by design, not by default. The power comes from how you handle change.

Traditional change management has long focused on aligning people and processes to achieve continuous improvement. However, this approach no longer suffices to keep organizations competitive. Modern organizations now face two additional challenges: managing transformation and maintaining stability. These challenges require a more nuanced understanding of what to change and what to keep constant.

Traditional change management has focused on making gradual, incremental improvements—a steady, sometimes bureaucratic process that aims to align people, processes, and systems.

Traditional change management focuses on the alignment of people, processes, and systems to move the organization forward in a steady, linear fashion. It assumes that with the right amount of planning and communication, change will occur smoothly over time. While this approach promotes consistency, it often prioritizes maintaining the status quo over innovation and can hinder agility in fast-changing environments.

The modern version of change management integrates transformation management and stability management— two complementary forces that allow organizations to not only adapt rapidly but also protect their core strengths.

Transformation Management

Transformation management deals with managing accelerated change. This approach is necessary when the pace of external conditions demands significant leaps to catch up and stay ahead, as opposed to gradual, continuous adjustments. This type of change is strategic, financial, and cultural. Unlike traditional change management, which seeks to optimize existing processes, transformation management involves a fundamental rethinking of an organization's core.

Transformation happens when market dynamics or internal challenges create conditions that can no longer be supported by incremental changes. It can be triggered by technological disruptions, market realignment, or shifts in economic conditions. These scenarios demand a profound shift in the way a company operates—from its processes and people to its culture and financial structures. Transformation is not a series of small steps but rather a decisive jump to reposition the organization in their new reality.

Take a legacy retail company for example. As foot traffic declines and online shopping becomes the new status quo, they decide to pivot to a digital first approach after years of relying on brick-and-mortar stores. This change requires transformation. The store's business model, customer engagement strategy and internal culture all need to be reshaped. This change would be driven by new technologies, necessitating a cultural shift toward agility and innovation, as well as strategic investments that align the organization with its new goals.

Transformation management requires bold leadership. It involves managing uncertainty, navigating through strategic realignment, and rapidly integrating new technologies and systems while inspiring the workforce to embrace the new direction.

Stability Management

On the other side of the equation lies stability management. Stability management deals with determining what must remain consistent in an organization to ensure it remains competitive without becoming bureaucratic or idle. The goal is to safeguard the core values, structures, and processes that contribute to an organization's success, while still allowing room for innovation and change.

Stability management establishes that not everything needs to change. In fact, some things must stay the same to maintain continuity, efficiency, and competitive advantage. This is particularly important for mature organizations that have built successful operations but could still be disrupted by sudden changes. Stability is not resistance to change, but rather a deliberate choice to protect the organization's working pillars that ensure long-term viability.

Take, for instance, a company with a strong, well-established brand in the marketplace. The stability of their brand identity should remain intact, even as the company innovates and modernizes. To ensure this, the organization must determine what contributed to their current reputation and success, and work towards incorporating those fundamental processes into and alongside the new plan.

Similarly, operational efficiencies developed over years of refinement shouldn't be discarded hastily in the pursuit of transformation. Stability management helps to ensure that these essential elements provide a solid foundation for future changes.

The art of stability management lies in defining which pillars are essential and must stay consistent, while still maintaining flexibility to evolve in other areas. This balance prevents the organization from becoming overly rigid or resistant to necessary change, avoiding the pitfalls of stagnation and inefficiency.

Recipe for Success: The Balance of Transformation and Stability

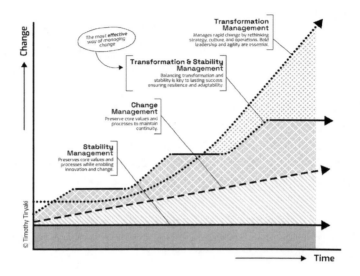

The key to successful change management lies in balancing transformation and stability. Transformation management drives the necessary leaps that allow organizations to adapt to disruptive forces, while stability management safeguards the essential elements that ensure continuity and efficiency. When used together, these approaches create a dynamic equilibrium—allowing organizations to evolve without losing sight of their core strengths. By maintaining stability in foundational areas while embracing transformative shifts where needed, organizations can navigate complex environments and remain competitive. Leaders must understand that lasting success depends on using both forces in tandem to create an adaptable yet resilient organization.

Lifecycle Considerations

Organizations must use these two change management approaches together, but where an organization lies in its lifecycle heavily influences the emphasis on transformation or stability management. For a startup, transformation is often a constant need, as the company rapidly scales and adapts to new market conditions. In contrast, a mature organization will likely need to focus on stability management to preserve the competitive advantages it has built over time, while also strategically introducing change.

Transformation may be essential in periods of significant industry shifts or disruptions, but stability becomes key as an organization matures and seeks to sustain its growth and market position. A clear understanding of the organization's life cycle allows leaders to balance these two forces effectively, ensuring transformation and stability are each applied when necessary.

Organizations need more than traditional change management. By integrating transformation and stability management, leaders can create a framework that supports both rapid adaptation and the preservation of critical strengths. The ability to discern what should change and what should remain stable empowers organizations to thrive amid evolving challenges and opportunities.

At Maslow Research Center, we help organizations strike this balance, ensuring they are ready for both the present and the future. In our culture consulting practice, we identify both the transformation agenda while exploring the stability anchors the organization needs.

Bringing Coaching into Culture Transformation: Organizational Culture Coaching©

In conversations with several Fortune 500 companies during culture transformation projects, as well as conversations with coaches and other leaders, I have heard numerous times that implementation is the missing piece. A lot of money, time, and energy goes into the analysis, strategy, and alignment, yet companies frequently lack the implementation support.

It's usually quite expensive for consultants to follow through and create real change, and leaders or managers are not always equipped either. Having noticed this gap, instead of an advisory approach, I have proposed bringing a coaching approach into culture transformation.

With this, I defined a new field in coaching called Organizational Culture Coaching©. Since 2020, I have been defining and pioneering this field both with research and practice. I have presented OCC at various global coaching conferences and invited researchers, practitioners, and industry experts to collaborate on this field. We've developed an ability to support culture analytics and coach leaders and managers through the implementation of what we call culture action plans.

Culture action plans are different than regular action plans. Many managers are good at action planning. They understand the technical side of action planning: who's responsible, who's accountable, who supports who, and who informs who. Unfortunately, the typical action plan templates frequently become static, and the survey ends up being a once a year a survey that has no follow through. The biggest missing link of typical actions plans is that they don't address a mindset shift, nor do they identify how leaders can role model culture.

However, we've developed a culture action planning canvas, which evolved through human-centered design thinking processes. I had a chance to prototype and improve this approach with several organizations. The healthiest process we've developed to help organizations work on culture is to build a baseline by measuring culture using the Culture-Actualization Index©, communicating results, conducting executive alignment, and starting to build culture action plans.

This requires facilitation at multiple levels; when the culture action plans are built, the real work starts. Leaders need to receive ongoing coaching once or twice a month to be sure they're held accountable and capable for their culture action plans.

We know that leaders make it or break it, and that people join companies but leave managers. We need to be sure that leaders are role modeling the change we want to see, and that happens by having a safe space to reflect with a coach to understand what's working or not. Culture coaches can aid in customizing the culture action plan and keeping the leader accountable. Even better, they can implement a process that we call shadow coaching or field coaching; this is where the coach spends time on the ground with the manager and the team gets to witness. The behavioral observation of what's happening offers great feedback and development opportunities.

This field of Organizational Culture Coaching© happens through trained coaches who understand leadership dynamics and workplace culture dynamics that help the leader lead with culture.

Implementation coaching is one of the key aspects of making a culture change, and a transformation of success. Leaders don't need constant consulting; it's not about constant advice. It's about coaching to empower them to lead with culture.

The Maslow Culture Transformation Roadmap

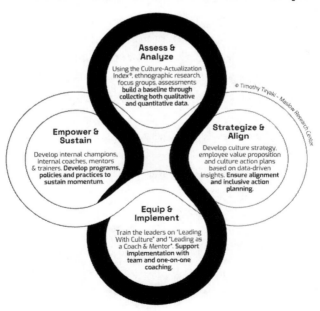

Assess & Analyze

Using the Culture-Actualization Index©, ethnographic research, focus groups, assessments **build a baseline through collecting both qualitative and quantitative data.**

© Timothy Tiryaki - Maslow Research Center

Empower & Sustain

Develop internal champions, internal coaches, mentors & trainers. **Develop programs, policies and practices to sustain momentum.**

Strategize & Align

Develop culture strategy, employee value proposition and culture action plans based on data-driven insights. **Ensure alignment and inclusive action planning.**

Equip & Implement

Train the leaders on "Leading With Culture" and "Leading as a Coach & Mentor". **Support implementation with team and one-on-one coaching.**

If we want to build both people-focused and high-performing organizations, we need to find better ways of understanding and measuring workplace culture.

To do this, we need to educate leaders on how to lead with culture. We need to bring shared language and educate them on their toolkits and culture management competencies. This can be done through educating leaders on understanding culture as employee experience and, hence, building familiarity with employee needs. This way leaders can ask questions, listen, and understand the employees better.

We can also bring in a culture measure to create a baseline score, which can be improved on and used as an on-going KPI. The Culture-Actualization Index© measures culture as employee experience. We can also call it the Employee Experience Index. The Index creates a baseline for understanding how much you are meeting your employees' basic needs, psychological needs, and growth needs. The Operational Culture Index© takes this a step further and analyzes how the company's operations are shaping the workplace culture, and where the disconnects are.

These research-driven frameworks help your leaders at all levels build a shared language on the changing workplace dynamics, and how to lead with culture.

Measuring Culture

One of the biggest challenges of organizations is attracting and retaining talent. The Great Resignation of the post-Covid-19 era has taught us that employees will leave their employers if their individual and collective needs are not met.

Measuring culture is a complex and challenging task. Some don't believe we can measure culture. Comparably, one could look at measuring an intricate and multifaceted topic like love. An initial attempt of quantifying love could count the number of hugs and kisses, or "I love yous" in a day, but will soon uncover that these actions may not reflect genuine feelings on an individual level. I do agree that some things cannot be fully measured. Yet as sample sizes increase, we are able to observe shared patterns of behaviors. The Gottman Index, for example, is a scientifically validated and widely accepted way of understanding how the behaviors between couples will lead to a more fulfilled marriage or one that might end up unsuccessful.

Just like measuring genuine love, accurately gauging the impact and importance of culture requires a nuanced and in-depth understanding of its complexities. However, this should not discourage us from seeking ways to measure culture. Instead, it should only prompt us to investigate further, understand the different facets of culture, and explore which facets of it we could use as a performance indicator.

The current measures that are used for culture describe employee engagement or trust levels. These engagement surveys were developed twenty to thirty years ago. They do not capture the new workplace dynamics. We need a new way to understand, measure, and educate our leaders on workplace culture.

As I have already revealed, workplace culture can be defined through culture as a North Star, culture as an operational fabric, and culture as employee experience. I believe the biggest gap in understanding is with employee experience hence why I started this research from there. This book summarizes our research findings on understanding culture as employee experience, by understanding employees' needs, and the findings were used to develop the Culture-Actualization Index©. It also explores our research on culture as operational fabric, and the Operational Culture Index© derived from it. These index measures show very high levels of reliability and predictability, and we encourage organizations to start using these measures as a key performance indicator (KPI) for culture.

As we continue to explore culture as a North Star, my vision is to develop one of the most comprehensive ways of looking at workplace culture. We are continuously seeking organizations to partner with and continue our research.

The approach in this book proposed that organizations can reach their full potential when they see culture as employee experience and consider their employees' basic, psychological, and growth needs and by also considering how operations influence culture. The aim is to build high-performing teams and a people-focused culture by actively leading with culture. Our research confirmed that the Culture-Actualization Index© and the Operational Culture Index© are not only a reliable way to measure an organization's culture, but that the scores can predict other organizational outcomes including work engagement, job satisfaction, and turnover. It allows leaders to acknowledge that employees have unique needs and provides specific insight for addressing those needs. Using the Culture-Actualization Index©, we can determine which leaders are effectively coaching, mentoring, and role modeling for their team's growth needs. We can also identify areas where employees are lacking psychological safety or where their basic needs are not being met.

Coupled with The Operational Culture Index©, these tools give you a comprehensive toolkit to measure multiple facets of workplace culture. The data offers specific insight that can empower organizations to build a more supportive and engaging workplace culture, ultimately leading to more committed and satisfied employees. The power to create a great workplace culture is at your fingertips—all you need to do is measure it! And the goal is to keep getting at least 1% better each and every year.

Understanding A Role Model Organization

Imagine a company where, on the first day of work, a new employee is greeted not with a stack of forms, but with a personalized welcome experience. From the moment they arrive, the tools and technology they need to succeed are already set up, working seamlessly.

Their manager ensures that they have the training necessary to navigate both the tools and the culture, leaving no room for frustration or feeling left behind.

Onboarding at this company is comprehensive. Each employee is introduced to their role with clarity, and more importantly, they are given a deep understanding of the company's purpose and how their work contributes to it.

During the first week, they meet colleagues from across departments, fostering connections and camaraderie that establishes an essential foundation for collaboration. The organization's culture of inclusivity shines, as diverse voices are actively encouraged and genuinely valued from day one.

In this organization, employees know that their job security is taken seriously. Open communication about the company's future and their individual role within it creates a sense of stability. Employees feel fairly compensated and know that the benefits they receive—from healthcare to parental leave—are competitive and designed with their well-being in mind.

As they settle into their workspace, they find a safe, clean, organized, and creative environment where ideas flow freely. Whether brainstorming in dedicated spaces or collaborating with others, they feel supported by the layout and the resources available to nurture innovation.

Every day, well-being is prioritized. The company offers flexible work hours, encourages taking breaks, and provides access to fitness programs and mental health resources. Work-life balance isn't just a phrase here—it's a reality. Employees don't feel pressured to sacrifice their health for productivity. Because of the organization's commitment to their well-being, employees willingly contribute during busy periods or demanding work cycles, doing so with dedication.

Employee consideration is deeply embedded in this company's policies and practices. Feedback loops are constant, and leadership regularly reviews how well policies meet the actual needs of the workforce. It's clear that this company listens to its people, adjusting when necessary to ensure that the day-to-day realities align with broader organizational goals.

When challenges arise, the psychological safety cultivated within the company allows employees to speak up without fear. Whether it's raising concerns about workplace safety or suggesting improvements in team dynamics, every voice is heard. The leaders not only encourage inclusive decision-making but also actively practice it, showing that they value input from every corner of the organization.

The company's leaders role model its values every day. They show employees what integrity looks like in action, ensuring that they don't just preach values—they live them. Clear, consistent goal setting is the norm, and employees always understand what's expected of them and how their work ties into the company's larger mission.

Employees are not only mentored but also coached toward their potential. Leaders believe in their people, offering regular constructive feedback that inspires growth rather than fear. Managers here don't just provide oversight; they actively listen to their employees, ask thoughtful questions, and encourage them to push their boundaries, knowing that the organization is behind them every step of the way.

At this company, belonging is palpable. Every individual feels like they are an integral part of the team, not just a cog in a machine. The relationships they build here—with peers, mentors, and leaders—form the foundation of a strong community, where collaboration is the rule rather than the exception.

Finally, as employees reflect on their experience at this role model company, they realize that it's more than just a workplace—it's a community built on trust, shared purpose, and a genuine commitment to employee growth. This is a company that has mastered the art of leading with culture, where people feel fulfilled, engaged, and inspired to contribute their best every single day.

As you began reading, you might have felt that this vision sounds ideal—perhaps thinking, "Exactly, this is how work should be!" But as you progressed, it may have started to feel utopian and unrealistic. I hear you. No organization scores 100% on all these dimensions all the time. Still, that doesn't diminish the vision of what leading with culture is and should strive to be.

I want to remind you that all organizations that lead with culture or focus on building great workplace cultures have something in common—they keep culture on their agenda. Workplace culture is something you continually cultivate. It requires deliberate attention, education for your leaders and your people, and ongoing effort. Think of culture like a garden. You try to do everything you can to maintain a healthy ecosystem, like watering every area evenly. But you'll notice that different parts of the garden receive varying amounts of sunlight, the soil composition changes, and some areas will face more weeds or pests. Some spots will thrive naturally.

This is where a dynamic approach comes in—you begin to speak the language of your garden. While you observe the individual plants, flowers, and trees, you develop a deeper understanding of the garden as a whole.

As you bring the leading with culture approach into your organization, you must continuously evaluate the top three to five areas of focus each year. You'll improve in some areas, and in others, you may regress. You may find that a practice you excelled at ten years ago has now fallen lower on the list, or that something which used to be a challenge is now one of your strengths—a sign that past initiatives were successful.

The key is to seek that 1% improvement continuously, to listen to the whole organization—the organism—and sense what's happening. Through ongoing diagnostics, you can measure and develop the capabilities necessary to proactively manage the health of your organization.

I invite all of you to reflect on the deep connections between leadership and culture, and to recognize how intertwined they truly are. If you understand the paradigm shift from viewing the organization as a well-oiled machine to seeing it as a living organism—where we, including the leaders, are the cells of the body, each interdependent—you are one step closer to leading with culture.

I hope this book broadens your perspective as a leader. I encourage each reader to take one small, meaningful step toward contributing to this vision. Thank you for reading and being part of this journey.

References

Clifton, J., & Harter, J. K. (2019). It's the Manager: Gallup finds the quality of managers and team leaders is the single biggest factor in your organization's long-term success. Washington, DC, USA:: Gallup Press.

Clifton, J., & Harter, J. (2021). Wellbeing at work. Simon and Schuster.

De Smet, A., et al. (2023). Some Employees Are Destroying Value, Others Are Building It—Do You Know the Difference? McKinsey & Company. Retrieved from https://www.mckinsey.com/capabilities/people-and-organizationalperformance/our-insights/some-employees-are-destroying-value-others-are-building-it-do-you-know-the-difference

Gardner, H. (1993). Multiple intelligences: The theory in practice. Basic books.

Goleman, D. (1998). Working with emotional intelligence. Bantam.

Goleman, D. (2011). The brain and emotional intelligence: New insights (Vol. 94). Northampton, MA: More than sound.

Hartner, J., & Pendell, R. (2021, September 9). Is the 4 Day Work Week a Good Idea? Gallup. Retrieved from https://www.gallup.com/workplace/342299/four-day-work-week-good-idea.aspx

Harter, J. (2023). Employee Engagement Needs to Rebound in 2023. Gallup. Retrieved from https://www.gallup.com/workplace/468233/employee-engagement-needs-rebound-2023.aspx

Microsoft. (2021). The Next Great Disruption is Hybrid Work—Are We Ready? Microsoft Work Trend Index Annual Report. Retrieved May 3, 2023, from https://www.microsoft.com/en-us/worklab/work-trend-index/hybrid-work

Microsoft. (2021). Microsoft Work Trend Index. Retrieved from https://www.microsoft.com/en-us/worklab/work-trend-index/hybrid-work

World Economic Forum. (2021). What is the great resignation and what can we learn from it? Retrieved from https://www.weforum.org/agenda/2021/11/what-is-the-great-resignation-and-what-can-we-learn-from-it/

Appendix A

The Culture-Actualization Index© Research
Round One: Qualitative Research

We began our research with two goals in mind: to understand the new employee needs framework that integrates Maslow's Hierarchy of Needs in the context and understanding of the post-Covid-19 era, and to develop a tool that measures workplace culture as employee experience from a needs perspective.

We conducted our initial round of qualitative research in April 2020, which spanned a period of fifteen months amid the Covid-19 pandemic. This allowed us to capture and frame the changing needs at work at a crucial time and gain insight into how the pandemic was changing the workplace.

We conducted 10 focus groups with 120 participants, all of whom were leaders of mid-sized and large organizations across North America, to ask them their understanding of culture and needs in the workplace.

With the data from these focus groups, we conducted cluster analyses, which is the process of attributing closely related concepts discovered in their responses. By looking at the frequency of used terms, we were able to identify themes and create concept clusters that formed the foundation for the development of Culture-Actualization 1.0, or the Human Needs at Work©, framework.

Culture-Actualization 1.0 was based on the original five main dimensions of Abraham Maslow's framework (physiological, safety, love and belonging, esteem, and self-actualization needs), while incorporating cultural layers and 21st century workplace context to make it relevant to our experience today. Our findings and cluster analyses confirmed that there were three dimensions of needs at work: six clusters of basic needs, six clusters of psychological needs, and six clusters of growth needs. This aligned with a previous redesign of Maslow's framework done by Clayton Alderfer, who organized needs into the ERG Model (Existential Needs, Relational Needs, Growth Needs) to simplify Maslow's framework to cluster the basic and psychological needs, further confirming our findings.

In Culture-Actualization 1.0, the first cluster of basic needs included technology, training, rewards, physical wellbeing, and environment. Surrounding these were the psychological needs identified as needs of inclusion, social connection, collaboration, learning and development, and recognition. The third level was the growth needs, where one must be in a people-focused environment where people are empowered, where leadership is cohesive, and where leaders take a coach-and-mentorship approach.

After this first phase of research, we concluded that meeting all three basic, psychological, and growth needs at work outlined by the 1.0 framework is necessary to reach culture-actualization.

After we developed the Culture-Actualization 1.0 framework, we were keen to put it to the test. To prototype our model, we conducted ten half-day workshops with organizations from different industries. We shared the findings and asked the participants to further discuss what they needed from their workplace, from each other, and from their leaders.

The common language proved very powerful, as once people found the right language to express their needs, we observed that they experienced a powerful sense of connection and cohesion. Given these observations, we were confident we had a solid foundation for needs at work. We decided we needed to dig deeper and further understand what was happening in this framework. We applied for research grants with Mitacs, and started partnering with St. Mary's University's Organizational Psychology department.

Research Round Two: Quantitative Research

After we received the grant, and under the supervision of a reputable behavioral scientist and professor, we started working on the development of the quantitative index.

As a first step, we conducted a literature review to better understand what other research had been done in the field and what other tools were being used to evaluate workplace culture. We discovered that there was no other survey based on Maslow's Hierarchy of Needs to relate to, or directly evaluate, organizational culture. There were many organizational culture surveys and one individual survey that focused on Maslow's principles, but the literature review revealed that the concept and approach was a new contribution to the field.

Phase 1

We looked back at our qualitative research and revisited the statements. From the original insights as well as our continued data collection, a list of eighty-nine items was developed to represent the basic, psychological, and growth needs. Once we had clearly defined them and their categories, we reached out to subject matter experts and began content validation, the process of confirming that we had accurately captured the underlying concept of workplace needs and culture. Through two rounds of subject matter consultation, HR leaders and business leader experts were asked their professional opinions on the statements and whether they agreed with the chosen category.

With their feedback, we conducted another round of expert reviews with organizational psychology PhD students to include their perspective and expertise in human behavior in organizations. These individuals engaged in a sorting task that removed statements that were not conceptually consistent, further refining the list of items. Items that were sorted correctly 75% or more of the time were kept for further analysis, while the rest were deemed no longer relevant due to poor content validity. Other items were eliminated if they were hard to understand, double-barreled, nonrepresentative, or redundant. This process resulted in a significant reduction of items, from eighty-nine to fifty-three.

Phase 2

The second phase of our research project aimed to confirm the psychometric properties of the Culture-Actualization Index© to determine its reliability and validity. For this purpose, we conducted a two-wave study consisting of two surveys (or waves) released to participants one month apart.

To get the most robust data, participants had to work at least thirty-five hours a week, be over the age of eighteen, and have a direct supervisor. We also ensured that our sample size was well-distributed to accurately represent the North American sample. In the future, we aim to conduct further research focusing on specific groups (age, industry, gender) in North America and across Europe to continue our understanding of how the Hierarchy of Needs applies in the workplace and how it varies amongst different groups.

The two-wave study allowed us to collect additional data and confirm the reliability of the survey. In total, 404 individuals responded.

After the second survey had concluded, analysis began. The first step was an exploratory factor analysis, which was conducted to understand the components of the Culture-Actualization Index© and further eliminate any irrelevant or inaccurate items. The second wave was conducted to confirm convergent validity. This assessed if our measure was on par with other measures looking at the same concepts. The third step was completed to confirm predictive validity, which assessed if the Culture-Actualization Index© could predict organizational outcomes. The last step of the analysis was performed to test the survey's reliability, ensuring that it was measuring what it was intended to, and to evaluate how the survey scores changed over time.

Convergent Validity

The analysis revealed that the Culture-Actualization Index© strongly related to measures of similar constructs, demonstrating that it was on par with other industry leading surveys. For example, basic needs were compared to the Rewards Satisfaction Scale (De Gieter et al., 2009), which is similar in that they measure the rewards and benefits offered in an organization.

Reliability

The analysis showed an exceptionally high level of reliability, confirming that the Culture-Actualization Index© was testing what it was intended to. The survey was also deemed to produce moderately stable results over time. This aligned with our expectation to properly represent changes in an organization's workplace culture over time.

Predictive Validity

The analysis concluded that higher scores on the Culture-Actualization Index© were directly related to higher scores in trust, psychological safety, creativity, work engagement, job satisfaction, organizational commitment, and job performance in the organization. It also concluded that high culture-actualization is correlated to lower turnover.

Appendix B

The Operational Culture Index© Research

The research for this project aimed to understand how the operations of an organization shape its workplace culture. The Operational Culture Index© (OCI) was developed to complement the Culture-Actualization Index© (CAI), forming a comprehensive toolkit for measuring culture holistically. While the CAI focuses on culture from the perspective of employee needs, the OCI evaluates it through the lens of organizational operations. This research aimed to validate the OCI and expand our set of cultural measurement tools. It also examined the interplay between the OCI and CAI, analyzing how their unique focuses influence different outcomes over time.

<u>Phase 1</u>

Our understanding of operational culture developed through years of observing how team communication and employee experience impact operational efficiency. This insight led to the creation of the Operational Culture Levers© framework, which encompasses eight factors:

strategy, structure, decision-making, leadership, people, processes, policies/practices, and systems.

Since 2020, these eight levers have been central to our workshops, evolving into the foundation of the Operational Culture Index© research. Through subject matter expert consultation, each lever was distilled into measurable statements. In total, forty-three statements were produced from this process and placed into the eight categories.

From here, we conducted a content validation study to ensure that the statements accurately measured the eight factors. Ten subject matter experts, including Industrial/Organizational Psychology graduate students and professionals with experience in organizational development, strategy, and human resources, participated in the study. Their role was to evaluate the relevance of each item to its respective factor. This process led to the final survey being refined to 27 items, and the experts concluded that these items accurately captured the intended constructs. The experts' feedback was then further used to clarify the survey language, ensuring that the final version was clear, concise, and relevant. This content validation study provided evidence that the Operational Culture Index© is an accurate measure of the eight key factors of organizational culture.

Phase 2

Phase two encompassed the psychometrics portion of the research process. Much like the CAI research, this contained a two-wave study and aimed to further develop and validate the OCI.

Two surveys, including all OCI and CAI items and a series of additional measures, were launched one month apart. Respondents were gathered from the online survey panel Prolific and had to meet the same requirements as the CAI research surveys; be 18 years or older, have a direct supervisor, and work a minimum of 35 hours each week.

The first survey had 368 respondents. Of that group, 275 participated in the second survey. The first survey collected the demographics of respondents and again, we ensured that our sample size was well-distributed to accurately represent the North American sample. Here are some specifics: there were 187 females, 174 males and 4 participants who identified as a different gender. This group had a high proportion of formally educated individuals, most of whom had a Bachelor's degree. The median length of time they had been with their organization was 5.63 years.

Exploratory Factor Analysis

Much like the CAI, once the data was gathered, we conducted an exploratory factor analysis. This process was used to further investigate the structure of the measure, understand how the statements related to each other, and remove items if they did not relate. This step of the research process reduced our categories to three: structure, people, and systems. It further reduced the statements in those categories to 10 relevant statements. Statements were removed for two reasons; if they were too broad and fit into more than one category or conversely, if they were unrelated to the other factors.

Convergent Validity

This step assessed whether our measure was on par with other measures looking at the same construct. Each category (structure, people, systems) was tested against another valid and reliable measure to ensure that it was closely related while still maintaining its uniqueness. The analysis concluded that our three factors reflected similarities with their comparisons, indicating consistency in measuring their intended constructs.

Reliability

The OCI had high reliability scores. This was tested in two ways; by analyzing the stability of the survey responses at two different points in time (test-retest reliability), and by assessing if the survey items consistently measured the intended constructs (internal reliability). The research found that the OCI scores from survey one could significantly predict the scores from survey two. It also found that the survey consistently measured the intended facets of organizational culture. These findings indicate that the tool is stable and reliable over time.

Predictive Validity

Predictive validity assesses how well a measure predicts future outcomes or behaviors. A correlation analysis indicated that high OCI scores correlated with high scores of creativity at work, job satisfaction, work engagement, and loyalty within an organization. It also showed a moderate correlation with trust in the organization and organizational commitment, and a weak positive correlation with job performance. Notably, we also found that the OCI has a moderate negative relationship with turnover, meaning that higher OCI scores are associated with lower turnover rates. A subsequent regression analysis confirmed the OCI's moderate to high predictive power.

Phase 3

In Phase 3 of our study, we explored the relationship between the Operational Culture Index© (OCI) and the Culture-Actualization Index© (CAI) using correlational analysis, exploratory factor analysis, and longitudinal regression techniques. This comprehensive approach provided insights into how the two indices align, differ, and influence organizational outcomes over time.

Correlation Analysis

This step assessed the strength and direction of the relationship between the OCI and CAI. A strong positive correlation was observed at both time points, showing that as OCI scores increase, CAI scores follow suit, indicating that both indices reflect similar aspects of organizational culture. This consistent relationship over time confirms their alignment and underscores their effectiveness in evaluating organizational culture.

Exploratory Factor Analysis

This analysis was used to uncover the underlying structure of the OCI and CAI, as well as their similarities and differences, by grouping related items into factors.

The findings suggest that the two indices capture complementary elements of organizational culture but are unique in what they specifically measure. This means that each index focuses on different dimensions, and their combined use offers a more comprehensive view of organizational culture. The distinct factors highlight that neither index alone fully captures all cultural aspects, but together, they provide a more detailed and holistic evaluation.

Longitudinal Analysis

The longitudinal regression analysis aimed to understand how the two culture surveys interact and evolve over time, revealing their independent and joint predictive power and identifying their unique contributions and areas of interconnectedness. The findings of this analysis further confirmed that the OCI and CAI should be used in tandem. It found that the OCI highlights current cultural strengths and weaknesses, while the CAI monitors the long-term impact and sustainability of cultural initiatives. With the added understanding of how both tools function over time, the assessment of organizational culture is increasingly holistic and nuanced.

As previously mentioned, the People category emerged as statistically significant in our research. However, due to the complexity surrounding its relationship with the Culture-Actualization Index©—which focuses on the human experience and leadership behaviors that directly impact employees—we opted to exclude it from the OCI survey. This decision allows us to conduct further research to better understand how the People factor in the Operational Culture Index© complements or diverges from the CAI, which will be explored in future iterations.

Future Research

Our research roadmap is towards building the most comprehensive way of understanding organizational culture in the 21st century. This means decoding the three facets of culture: the north star, the operational culture and the employee experience. Now that we have covered the latter two, we are moving into researching culture as north star in 2025. The North Star framework will bridge the gaps between the purpose, vision and values of the organization with strategy and culture. This tool will allow us to further understand how these different dimensions affect and interact with each other and will also add another dimension to our comprehensive approach to measuring organizational culture.

We are always looking for organizations who are early adopters interested in collaborating, partnering and using these tools in their workplace. Please reach out to us at Maslow Research Center if you want to implement the Leading with Culture© approach in your organization and help us continue developing our culture measurement tools.

Acknowledging Limitations

As a researcher, I appreciate skepticism. Many times, we have been asked: how can you be sure of your research findings? First, I want to recognize that this work is within social sciences, distinct from natural sciences like chemistry or physics. Unlike those natural sciences, where laws like that of gravity are uniform and apply equally to all parts of the world, the rules governing social phenomena are not fixed and can vary significantly across different cultures and societies. What works in one country may not work in another, and social norms and behaviors differ based on various factors including history, traditions, and values.

In fact, there can even be differences in Maslow's order of needs based on national culture. For example, some Scandinavian cultures consider belonging as being a higher need than esteem. Therefore, we cannot assume that the principles of social science have universal applicability, as they are highly context-dependent and subject to change. However, in our work, we apply scientific methodologies and statistical analyses to approach the data, much like the processes in other sciences. This solidifies that our research and data are scientific in nature, and highlights that the social context in which it is gathered creates varied results.

We acknowledge that what we're sharing is based on data collected from North American employees. Therefore, our findings are directly related to North American workplace culture. That said, in surveys that we have conducted in Europe, organizations have found the findings and research just as useful, indicating high alignment between the Culture-Actualization Index© and Anglo-Saxon culture.

Similar to the CAI, the OCI is also built on North American data. While we recognize that the research is North American centric, its applicability in the workplace has great potential to go beyond just one continent. We invite participants from other geographies to explore the differences and also leverage the Culture-Actualization Index© and the Operational Culture Index©. We are aware that all research has limitations and are curious about how our findings apply to various geographies.

About The Author

Dr. Timothy Tiryaki is a globally recognized thought leader in leadership and culture transformation, with over two decades of experience spanning multinational corporations, consulting, and academia. Trained as an Industrial Engineer, Timothy began his career at Procter & Gamble and worked at Intel, where he gained invaluable experience working in complex, high-performance environments. He later transitioned into consulting at Great Place to Work Inc., where he helped organizations build and sustain high-trust cultures. Timothy has led culture transformation projects for Fortune 500 companies and culture merger projects. Timothy is an ICF-accredited Professional Coach and holds seven coaching certificates in multiple coaching styles. He has trained and coached leaders from large organizations, including Army Special Operations, PEO and the Marine Corps.

As the founder of Maslow Research Center and co-founder of Strategy.inc, Timothy integrates his extensive experience with a research-driven, human-centered approach to leadership and strategy. He holds a PhD in Leadership Education and continues to develop innovative frameworks that bridge theory and practice, providing actionable insights for today's leaders. Known for his ability to simplify complex concepts, Timothy's forward-thinking keynote speeches, leadership education programs and executive coaching sessions have empowered leaders globally.

Made in United States
Troutdale, OR
12/06/2024

25973263R00111